Unmasking

the Secret Sins Within

(The Sins That So Easily Beset Us!)

Author: Prophetess Yolanda Lee~George

"Unmasking the Secret Sins Within"

Copyright © 2016 Black~Butterfly Publishing Inc.

All rights reserved. No part of this book may be reproduced, scanned, or distributed in any printed or electronic forms existing now or in the future without written permission from the publisher. For information regarding permission, please write to:
Black~Butterfly Publishing
www.yolovercome.com
yolovercome@yahoo.com

Please help in the fight against piracy of Copyrighted materials. Purchase only authorized editions.
ISBN-13: 978-0991076031
ISBN-10: 0991076036
All rights reserved. Published 2016.
Printed in the United States of America.

Book Design by: ENPS

Autograph Page

Dedication

I dedicate this book to the Holy Spirit, my leader, my guider, my comforter, my teacher, my all and all. The Holy Spirit ministered to me as I wrote this book.

I dedicate this book to all the silent voices that are out there, that may read this book. I stand as a voice for you in this season. I stand and expose the enemy of all the unhealthy, mind, body, soul and spirit eating sins that lay dormant within you; things that have held you hostage (in bondage) for many years and constipates the flow of the spirit within you.

I dedicate this book to the Overcomers; that will stay free from the tricks of the enemy, that you will stay healed, delivered and set free from the bondage of the Secret Sins that once held you hostage; I come to unmask the enemy and put him under our feet.

I pray right now in the Name of Jesus that everyone that reads this book, they will find peace that surpasses all understanding; that they will release their voices as the sound of a trumpet and silence the enemy in their ears.

No more shackles no more chains, no more bondage you are free!!! Amen

Acknowledgments

To my children **Nijah, Johnna, Johntavia, Johnavia** and **John III**; thank you for believing in me, trusting in me and being the people I practice on. Thank you for allowing me to Minister to you FIRST! My 7 grandbabies**Nijon, Nija'e, Na'Zariyah, Heaven, Ni'Asia, Josiah** and **John'tae(#8 sex is still unknown)** ☺ I love you all!

My husband**Lorenzo George, Sr.**thank you for respecting the call that God has placed upon my life, that causes me to expose my personable self to the world.

My number one fan, my dad, **Raymond Lee, Sr.,** my inspiration in life. I love you with every beat of my heart. Thank you for teaching me to be strong in the midst of the storms. I love you so very much!

My Sissy, **Felecia "Cookie" Lee**, thank you for pushing me and always believing in me! Girl you ROCK!

My Spiritual Sissy **Elder Lenora Claybore~Brown**,thank you for assisting in editing this book! I appreciate and love you to infinity!!! Muah

Angel Ferguson of Angel Ferguson Word-processing; thank you for always having my back and doing what God has anointed you to do. Thank you for your last minute 911 assistance!

Sis. Janice DuPree, THANK YOU for ALL your help right at 11:59 lol! You're amazing and I love you so much Sis!

Pastor Laytecia McKinney, my Spiritual Mother, I love and appreciate you for ALL that you pour into me. Thank you for the Foreword and for loving me unconditionally.

Table of Contents

Foreword – By Pastor Laytecia McKinney

Preface

Introduction

Chapter 1 – Spirits and Addictions

Chapter 2 – Debt Additions

Chapter 3 – Lying Spirit

Chapter 4 – Depression

Chapter 5 – Mental Dysfunction

Chapter 6 – Suicide

Chapter 7 - Pride

Chapter 8 – Hatred & Unforgiveness

Chapter 9 – Fear & Rejection

Chapter 10 – Doubt & Unbelief

Chapter 11 – Stubbornness & Rebellion

Chapter 12 – Jealous, Backbiting& Seeds of Discord

Chapter 13- Sex addiction (Incubus & Succubus)

Chapter 14 – Generational Curses

Foreword

In this must-read book: *"Unmasking the Secret Sins Within"*, Prophetess Yolanda Lee-George causes every reader to deal with the hidden sins that have been covered and buried with pride, and shame. She sets a foundation for deliverance, healing, restoration and liberty to all her readers.

Prophetess George is very candid in sharing her own personal journey, of how she was set free and delivered by the secret sins that held her bound and captive for many years. She conveys to her readers, that where you've been does not have to hinder you from where God wants to take you.

Is your past still hunting you within? Are you secretly sinning and hoping no one finds out? Do you have issues you never dealt with or overcome? Are you ready to be made whole? Are you ready to embrace ALL that God has for you? If you answered yes to any of those questions, then you need to read this book that will shift your life to the next dimension!

This book is designed to give you the keys to freedom from secret sins within!

Pastor Laytecia McKinney

Senior Pastor | Author

www.myvictorytemple.org | 5819 N. 56th Street | Tampa, FL | 33610

Preface

Unmasking the Secret Sins within
The Sins that so easily beset us

The Holy Spirit commissioned me to write this book, to be the voice for a mass body of believers that are being held captive by the enemy due to Secret Sins.

To share some of my my personal experiences, in order to help give others a voice. To be able to stand flat footed before the enemy and be able to say I'm delivered and you can't hold me captive by causing me to hide behind who I WAS and hindering me from being who I AM called to be by God.

Exposing sins that aren't always visible to the eyes so it's hidden! **BUT GOD!!!**

I pray this book will cause someone to go to the altar, to expose the enemy (not to anyone in particular, but even to yourself), to speak it out and renounce the enemy and claim the Lord Jesus Christ as your personal savior, knowing that you are healed. Amen

Introduction

Praise God to all my readers: Welcome as I invite you into my private life once again, to help others to unmask, overcome and not be ashamed of where they are, where they've been and what they need to overcome. I'll give you a brief into some very vital areas of sin that once held me captive in my own mind, emotions, body, soul and spirit...the secret sins that so easily beset me.

I need you to understand when I say secret sins, it's not JUST direct willful sins but some are considered sins because I allowed situations and things to hold me captive, such as my childhood and other things that are considered SIN, because I hid behind them and blocked the flow of God in my life.

I pray that this small piece of information will help direct you into your path of healing and to better understand thepower of spirits. I realize that this book **WILL NOT** give you everything you may need but I'm sure it's a start and that it will help someone as they read;I'm sure that someone will find themselves in my story. Amen

I can share this information because I've been delivered; I hid behind certain mask for over 34 years, fighting battles that I could not fight alone; ashamed to tell anyone what I was dealing with.At first I didn't even see it as a problem, I felt that it was just who I was. Please understand that we can't fight spirit with flesh *2 **Corinthians** 10:3-4 **SAYS:***For though we walk in the flesh, we do not war in the flesh: For the weapons of are warfare are not carnal, but mighty through God to the pulling down of strong holds. Therefore, understanding that we must fight spirit with spirit, there's no way we can fight a spirit with our own **incapable** flesh. Amen*

As I take you through this book of my life **YET AGAIN**, I'm going to try and make this book as understandable as I can and touch on as much as I can as the Holy Spirit gives me guidance and approval. Understanding that Sins, Strongholds and Addictions all run hand and hand. Amen
Sins: an offense against religious or moral law; an action that is or is felt to be highly reprehensible (it's a sin to waste food); an often-serious shortcoming or fault; transgression on Stronghold: an area dominated by a particular group (a group of demonic spirits that causes one to SIN against God) Addiction:

As I expose my private life to help assist someone else in unmasking and overcoming the secret sins that hold them in private bondage, sins that we all sometimes face; to overcome and expose the raw truth behind the enemy and the deceptive spirits that attached to us and cause us to be ashamed. No more shame, unmask the shame that the enemy has tried to hold you bound in and embrace life to the fullest. Your testimony can save someone else. So, let's go.PLEASE NOTE: SOME AREAS OF THIS BOOK IS NOT FOR MINORS TO READ – UNLESS APPROVED BY GUARDIAN – actually it's really not that deep!!! lol.

Disclaimer: Please note that I am aware that the language that is in this book IS NOT all grammatically correct, there will be some ain't, yeap, yeah etc. because I'm writing this book in my own voice (as I've done my other books). When people are going through certain situations in life, proper grammar is the last thing on their minds; when the Holy Ghost was giving this to me, HE did not give it to me caring about proper grammar. Amen

In this book, I'm very transparent, I'm able to unmask these secret sins because I've lived them and my daddy ABBA FATHER gave me permission to release and Unmask the Secret Sins. Everyone will **NOT** agree with what I'm saying and that's understandable, this is **STRICTLY** from MY own personal experiences and how I overcame.

I will be referencing some strongholds (family members) that come with one sin. We mustunderstand; these sins don't come alone.

Please read this book with the understanding that NO ONE is perfect, from the pulpit to the pews. Although delivered, it doesn't stop the enemy from trying to come back to see if there's any vacancies. Amen

CHAPTER 1

Spirits & Addictions they run hand and hand

Spirit: the force within a person that is believed to give the body life, energy, and power. A supernatural being or essence: as "Holy Spirit", an often malevolent being that is bodiless but can become visible; specifically: ghost. A malevolent being that enters and possess a human being. The activating or essential principle influencing a person, acted in a spirit of helpfulness.

Addiction: a strong and harmful need to regularly have something (such as a drug) or do something (such as gamble). An unusually great interest in something or a need to do or have something. Compulsive need for and use of habit-forming substance characterized by tolerance and by well-defined physiological symptoms upon withdrawal; broadly: persistent compulsive use of substance known by the user to be harmful.

As you can see, Spirits and Addictions work hand and hand, they're both strong influences and both take control of your being. As we go through these spirits and addictions (sins), some will be very short and to the point and some may take a few more lines. Amen ☺ I'll start with the basic ones and then go to the more difficult ones that really had me bound.

Prayer: Lord I pray as each person reads this book, that you will allow a spirit of deliverance to rush into their mind, soul, body and spirit that they will acknowledge and apply what could be holding them back from their next level of elevation. I pray that you bring these words alive in their spirit and that they will run to you and ask for forgiveness, healing and total deliverance, in the Name of Jesus! Amen!

CHAPTER 2

DEBT:

Debt: an amount of money that you owe to a person, bank, company, etc. the state of owing money to someone or something. Something owed, and obligation. The common-law action for the recovery of money held to be due.

People of God, please understand that debt is sin, that's why we pray the Lord's prayer, asking God to forgive us or debts as we forgive our debtors. Debt is a sin...Proverbs 22:26 Be not thou one of them that strike hands, or of them that are sureties of debts. Matthew 18:30 And he would not: but went and cast him into prison, till he should pay the debt.

When we get into a place where we are always borrowing, always needing something from others, and unable to pay it back OR we pay it back only to borrow it again; that's a problem, that's an addiction. I was in debt with Amscot for years. I ran into some issues and found out that it was easy to go through Amscot for a loan. People of God, please don't get entrapped with that bondage of borrowing from Amscot, yes, it's good for people that NEED it for something quickly, but when it becomes an addiction, there's a problem.

When I got in debt with Amscot, I thought it would be something quick and be done with it. I went to them and got that first $500, the interest on it was $50, so when I got paid, I had to take Amscot $550.00, but I quickly learned, that was the trap. When you borrow money (especially a large amount), you must remember that you must pay it back, with interest. I paid that first $550 and realized that my bills would be short yet again because I'd just released $550 that I didn't have. I quickly found myself going back 2 days later to get the $500 until my next pay day. Before I realized it, I was borrowing on the 3rd and 17th and paying back on the 1st and 15th when I got paid. Due to the fact, I wasn't able to just release a full $550 out of one check, that went on for a full year until income tax time. I'd pay it off during tax time and within 3 months I was back at Amscot doing the same thing all over again GETTING ANOTHER LOAN. Iwas poorly managing my money, spending carelesslyand found myself in debt to Amscot every year for 5 years back to back, paying them off during tax time and getting another loan with 1 to 3 months later because I'd be brokenyet again.

One day it's as if something hit me right before it was time for tax season. I realized that I had an addiction and it became an embarrassment that the people in the 3 Amscots I went to, they knew me by name, the reality was hard hitting. I cried out to God and realized that I had a problem, I was making Amscot rich and it was a set up from the beginning. I asked God to help me because this had to be a problem, the reality of having a problem like debt and not caring or at least thinking it didn't matter, was mind boggling; but I realized it was deeper than I thought I HAD AN ADDICTION. I cried out to God that when I paid these fees' off during tax season in 2013 to please help me manage my money, that I didn't want to ever in life be in debt or have to go to Amscot for anything for any reason. I asked God to show me how to put up money, to store monies and be a better stewardess over my money. I want to believe that, because I was a faithful tithes and offering payer, God sustained me even in my spending and debt ignorance.

When tax season came in 2013, I walked into Amscot to pay them off and said *"I will never come back again"* (now again, don't get me wrong; if you need it, please by all means use it, but if you can do without it and it's because you spent carelessly, please think twice because it's a trap from the enemy (AS FAR AS I'M CONCERENED), nevertheless, I was determined that when I walked out of Amscot that day, I wouldn't look back, and that by any means necessary I would NOT allow the enemy to send me back to that place. I would manage my money, that I would put up money, that I would hide money from myself, and use it for a purpose and this time I was going to learn how to save.

I must give God the glory, it's been 3 years since I've been to Amscot for a loan and I don't plan on going back. You must understand that borrowing had become a spiritual addiction, it was as if I needed to have that loan and still I was broke even with the loan. I refused to be in bondage of owing people and the Holy Spirit was my only source of getting made whole from the spirit of addiction from Amscot. I know to someone else this may seem very small but to someone else reading that's been there or there right now; they can relate and say Amen.

Prayer:I pray right now in the name of Jesus that this bit of information has helped someone realize that being in debt is a sin. I pray that the hands of the Lord and the guidance of the Holy Spirit, will cause you to ask for direction, ask for guidance in learning how to manage your finances and save. I pray a financial blessing over your lives and pray that debt will be pulled from the root of your spirit; leaving no residue...I declare and decree in the Name of Jesus that you're free from debit right now. I pray right now in the name of Jesus that you will lead and guide your people on how to get back on track with their finances, to help them to be better stewardess with their resources and finances. Amen, I pray this area of Debt has blessed someone. *YOU ARE DEBT FREE IN THE NAME OF JESUS!*

CHAPTER 3

Lying Spirits

Liar: a person that tells lies, a fabricator: to make up for the purpose of deception, **fibber:** an untrue statement about something minor or unimportant, **equivocate:** to use unclear language specially to deceive or mislead someone, dishonest: saying or likely to say things that are untrue, containing information that is untrue, used to deceive someone; **Untruthful**, unworthy of trust or belief, **Dishonest:** implies a willful perversion of truth in order to deceive, cheat, or defraud, to swindle. **(Ref. Webster Dictionary)**

Proverbs: 17:4 A wicked doer giveth heed to false lips; and a liar giveth ear to a naughty tongue. **KJV Bible**

Jeremiah 50:36 A sword is upon the liars; and they shall dote: a sword is upon her mighty men; and they shall be dismayed. **KJV Bible**

Proverbs: 6: 16-18 These six things doth the Lord hate: yeah, seven are an abomination unto him. A proud look, a lying tongue, and hands that shed innocent blood, a heart that deviseth wicked imaginations, feet that be swift in running to mischief. **KJV Bible**

There are many more scriptures that talk about lying spirits, because with a lying spirit will come other family memberswhich spirits are: Deception, Flattery, Religious, Bondages, Superstitions, Accusations, Gossip, Slander Etc.

I never in a million years considered myself a liar, I felt like I was a chick that kept it 100% as they say now. When I got saved it still took a while to confess that I was a liar and a good one at that. I felt because I didn't lie to people that was of importance to me, then it wasn't a lie because who cares about the ones on the outside…but a lie is a lie and it does not care who tells it. Amen

I realized I was actually a big liar, I lied to myself and I lied to other people, especially men. I felt like I didn't owe them an explanation about anything and I didn't owe them any truth, **WHO CARED**, I felt. God cared, and I was a liar. I'd lie to people at the flip of my tongue. So easily riding down the streets and someone yell my name, I'd yell out the window *"I'll be right back"* and I'd laugh to myself or whomever was with me saying *"Yeah right, I'm not going back over there"*. I'd tell people I was coming over and I knew that it wasn't true. I was downright willfully lying and didn't care or think anything of it. Men would ask if I was going to be home and I'd lie, my parents would ask me if I did such and such and I'd lie, because I was a liar. It's the small foxes that spoil the vines. It's those small quick, intentional lies that would keep me out of heaven as well.

I'm sure someone reading this is saying "Awe man, we all do that, that's nothing, that shouldn't count. Let's be honest…nowhere in the bible did it stipulate that we can tell certain lies and get away with it. LOL even I think to myself "geesh it's not that serious" but it is in the eyes of God, it's sin and that makes us no better than the thief.

I didn't want to hurt people's feelings but I had to learn (still have my days that I must catch myself), no is no and yes is yes. I'd rather hurt your feelings with the truth, than to hurt them with a lie.

There are times we tell these **little white lies** (as we call them, but there's not color to a lie in the eyes of God) but we tell them, just to spare someone's feelings; but at the end of the day, we're held at fault for our lie while we're making someone else feel good. We say yes to things we want to say no about, we tell people all sorts of lies just to make them feel good. Some even tell friends they look good in something that they know in their heart of hearts that it doesn't look good, but we don't want to hurt anyone's feelings HUMMM GOD SHOULD UNDERSTAND THAT RIGHT. No, the truth of the matter is, if the friend asks you a question and you are considered to be a true friend, you'd tell your friend the truth even if it hurts, because at the end of the day, your friend looks bad and you're feeling guilty for lying. If you don't know how to say it, quickly ask the Holy Ghost to give you wisdom and give your friend the heart to receive the truth.

I had to learn to just say what was the truth, I'm not turning back around, I don't feel like being bothered so don't come over, I don't have what you're asking me for at this moment OR I have it but I can't afford to let you get it right now. Just so many simple truths that could've rolled off my tongue but due to the fact I was telling quick simple lies, I was lying quite a bit and didn't even realize it yet I would say **"One thing about me, I'm not a liar"** but I felt that because things and people that meant something to me, I didn't lie to them…but again, a lie is a lie and a lie don't care who tells it.

I know personally of people who are pathological liars; they lie just to hold a conversation, they lie to your face when YOU know it's not the truth, they lie so much, they believe their own lies and will get upset about their lie because in their minds it's truth.

Lying is an ugly spirit and it causes division, it will cost you friends, family, jobs and can also cost you your life. Lying can cost you your marriage. Lying just to keep the peace is worse than just telling the truth and letting the other spouse get over it. I personally know someone that lies to their spouse all the time, they know certain situations WAY before the time and try to hit the other spouse with it at the last minute. When the other spouse ask WHY are they just finding out about the situation, they LIE and say they just found out and that's far from the truth. That will causedivision, and for some, it will cause them to lose trust.It causes one to look at your differently, especially when you tell lies that they know for a FACT you're lying about. You know how they say "women's intuitions" lol, we know you're lying and sometimes we'll say something and sometimes we just hold it and the proof as a trump card (which is not healthy either BUT it's what most females do).

For me, it's better to tell me the truth, let me be mad about the truth if that's what I want to do but at least I'm saying I'm mad about the truth compared to knowing that you've lied to me. That only makes if fester and cause resentment to set in; then you're walking around feeling some type of way within and never saying anything. Do you realize how many relationships are destroyed because of simple lies?

We quickly lie to our children without thinking twice about it OR we'll tell our children to tell someone a lie for us and then when the child lies to us, we want to break their necks. Amen

Confess that you're a liar and ask God to help you in that area, to purge your tongue to not lie, even what we call "little white lies" **A LIE IS A LIE!** Amen

Prayer: Father God we come to you right now in the name of Jesus asking that you remove every lying spirit from us. Lord we come against the spirit of deception that will try to cause us to be deceived and feel like our lies are truth. Your word says, let God be truth and every man a liar, so we cast down and break the back of the enemy that will try to destroy our purpose in you. I come against the spirit of a liar...Father we know that Satan is a liar, your words say in ***KJV John 8:44 You are of your father the devil, and the desires of your father you want to do. He was a murderer from the beginning, and does not stand in the truth, because there is not truth in him. When he speaks a lie, he speaks from his own resources, for he is a liar and the father of lies.*** In the name of Jesus, we pray. Amen

CHAPTER 4

Depression

Depression: (Oxford Dictionary) A common but serious mood disorder. Feelings of severe despondency and dejection "self-doubt creeps in and that swiftly turns to depression" A slump, recession, decline, downturn, standstill. (Mayo Clinic says) Depression is a mood disorder that causes a persistent feeling of sadness and loss of interest.

Again, most of us have experienced some form of depression in our lives for whatever reasons. To ME (**my personal opinion**) Depression and mental illness run hand and hand. I was depressed before my nervous breakdown; I was always down, felt bad about myself, always thinking I was ugly wasn't good enough, and felt worthless. I felt my husband (ex-husband now) didn't love me if he beat me the way that he did. He'd always tell me that I was fat and ugly, had 5 kids and no one would want me, then turn around and say I was beautiful REALLY.

I was sad all the time, I went to work, came home and went to church on days it was church. I wasn't fully functioning so when I had the nervous breakdown, I wasn't shocked. Felt like my life was going nowhere, like I was in a world wind and that's where I'd always be until I die.

I was depressed from my youth, but always had a fake smile on my face ***"Smiling faces tell lies"*** Amen! I was one of those people that smiled in front of my pain. My entire world could be crashing down around me but no one would know it because I always had a smile on.

Even church goers, we walk in the church and someone will ask how we're doing, we quickly LIE and say. *"I'm well, blessed and highly favored"*. That's not to say you're to tell everyone or just anyone your business but it is to say, get with someone that you can trust and release that mess, someone you can talk to and can say "**HELP, pray for me, I'm not doing good today**". Yes, I know some of you are saying "I'm not supposed to give the enemy praise, I'm not supposed to speak damnation over my own life, so I'm claiming joy, that's why I say I'm fine, or blessed and highly favored" but is that the truth or another lie? There's nothing wrong with saying, "I'm pressing my way BUT I know God is working in my favor" If it's someone you don't feel you want in your business, use wisdom and tell them "you'll be fine just continue to pray for me as I continue to pray for you" and let it be that. Nevertheless, don't sit in church and die on the pew or even in the pulpit. WHY SIT HERE TILL WE DIE. Amen

For those of you that are in church, and you have a Pastor that you don't trust enough to go into their office and release CHECK WHERE YOU'RE EATING FROM…You should be able to speak to your Pastor if not anyone else. If you're not in a church and you just feel you can't tell anyone or just don't trust anyone. You're going to have to learn how to lean, trust and depend on the Holy Ghost (WHICH SHOULD BE YOUR MAIN SOURCE ANYWAYS – BUT), realizing that the Holy Spirit is a person (the 3rd person in the trinity) and you can talk to the Holy Spirit and actually get a **response** "IF YOU'RE BEING STILL TO LISTEN" and lay at that altar until you get your break through instead of a break down, make an altar in your home, a place where you meet with the Lord. Bethel Amen

For me, I didn't trust anyone, on top of that I always portrayed the image as if I had it all together and I didn't want anyone to think otherwise, although I had an awesome support team (if I would've allowed them to be), my former Pastor was awesome, but due to **ME THINKING** *"my Pastor expects more out of me, He probably feels I should be elevated beyond these same hurts and pains* **ISSUES***, He's probably going to tell me to get over it"*. That was the enemy stopping me from going to my Pastor; maybe had I gone to him, I wouldn't have been in bondage as long as I was. So, I didn't go to him, I portrayed the image as if I was strong and had it all together. Yet I was screaming and dying inside, I was alone and felt I had no one or could trust anyone. I had to get to a place where I trusted God enough to appoint people in my life that I can trust, I had to get to a point that I could confide in someone, even if it was just a small amount that I released, that's why I ended up having a nervous breakdown because I held it all in.

I had to get to a place where I took responsibility, I had to accept the fact that I had to make some different choices; that some of the choices that I'd made in my life, had caused me some heartaches. I had to accept that I Yolanda, had caused quite a bit of the trials and tribulations that I was enduring because I didn't make proper choices and I was disobedience to the warning signs that was placed before me. I was taking on issues and situations of others that I had no business taking on and it felt like life was being drained from me and the weight of the world was on my shoulders.

We're depressed and overwhelmed with bad relationships, children, loneliness and feel as if no one else understands. We're trying to walk right in the Lord and our flesh needs a way of escape, but it's staying in HIS word and trusting Him. We get depressed because we're taking on things that's not ours to take on and we need to learn how to release and respect that "YOUR EMERGENCY IS NOT MY EMERGENCY! Amen

I had to also come to terms that I needed to trust God. I'd tried other stuff on my own and I'd failed and it was time to trust, lean and depend on God. As I always say, it was not easy to do and there are trials that I still face that I have to shake myself because I wonder if God is there even when I know that He is there BUT THIS OLE FLESH.

When God finally put certain individuals in my life and I begin to release a little of my heaviness, I started to feel a little better. No I still didn't give them my all but I could release some of the heaviness that weighed me down. I did get closer to God, got in the face of Him more and trusted HIM more. I started trusting the Holy Ghost, spending time in and with the Holy Spirit and allowing him to lead me.

I can say to you; you won't be disappointed if you try Him and trust Him. Never have I seen the righteous forsaken or His seed begging bread. Amen

Prayer: Father God in the Name of Jesus, I bind and cast out all spirits of depression, despondency, despair, discouragement, and hopelessness in the lives of your people in the name of Jesus, I pray, Amen

CHAPTER 5

Mental Illness

Mental Illness; it's a very touchy subject for me. I've had to deal with it personally with my ex-husband and I had to personally raise it, outside of dealing with my own issues. So, I took the time to search out some information that I pray is helpful to you. Amen

Mental Illness: (Merriam-Webster) any of a broad range of medical conditions (such as major depression, schizophrenia, obsessive compulsive disorder, or panic disorder) that are marked primarily by sufficient disorganization of personality, mind, or emotions to impair normal psychological functioning and cause marked distress or disability and that are typically associated with a disruption in normal thinking, feeling, mood, behavior, interpersonal interactions, or daily functioning.

I know there are different levels to Mental illness, such as it is for everything. I didn't experience mental illness on a level that others have and still do BUT I experienced it nonetheless.

Mental Illness/disorder, one tends to think it's just people that have severe issues, one's that have no self-control or just plain ignorant. That's far from the truth. There are people out there with a mental illness that you may never know they have a problem because it's under control. Mental illness doesn't take away from one's (not everyone at least) intelligence. There are people working in high places with mental illness, professional sports players with mental illnesses, Judges, Lawyers, Law Enforcement etc. with ADHD, ADD and other depression(my own word lol) mentalities.

Mental Illness is an imbalance of the *brain* **(PLEASENOTE):** *I'M NOT A PROFESSIONAL NOR DO I HAVE A DEGREE – but what I do have is personal experience, which is the best experience. Amen*

There are different causes for Mental Illness; I'll give you some information below that may better help you that I received from**(Reference:**

MedicineNet.com

http://www.medicinenet.com/mental_illness/article.htm)

Mental illness is any disease or condition that influences the way a person thinks, feels, behaves, and/or relates to others and to his or her surroundings. Although the symptoms of mental illness can range from mild too severe and are different depending on the type of mental illness, a person with an untreated mental illness often is unable to cope with life's daily routines and demands.

What Causes Mental Illness?

Although the exact cause of most mental illnesses is not known, it is becoming clear through research that many of these conditions are caused by a combination of genetic, biological, psychological, and environmental factors -- not personal <u>weakness</u> or a character defect -- and recovery from a mental illness is not simply a matter of will and self-discipline.

- **Heredity (genetics)**: Many mental illnesses run in families, suggesting they may be passed on from parents to children through genes. Genes contain instructions for the function of each cell in the body and are responsible for how we look, act, think, etc. However, just because your mother or father may have or had a mental illness doesn't mean you will have one. Hereditary just means that you are more likely to get the condition than if you didn't have an affected family member. Experts believe that many mental conditions are linked to problems in multiple genes -- not just one, as with many diseases -- which is why a person inherits a susceptibility to a mental disorder but doesn't always develop the condition. The disorder itself occurs from the interaction of these genes and other factors -- such as psychological trauma and environmental stressors -- which can influence, or trigger, the illness in a person who has inherited a susceptibility to it.

- **Biology**: Some mental illnesses have been linked to an abnormal balance of brain chemicals called neurotransmitters. Neurotransmitters help nerve cells in the brain communicate with each other. If these chemicals are out of balance or are not working properly, messages may not make it through the brain correctly, leading to symptoms of mental illness. In addition, defects in or injury to certain areas of the brain also have been linked to some mental conditions.
- **Psychological trauma**: Some mental illnesses may be triggered by psychological trauma suffered as a child, such as severe emotional, physical, or sexual abuse; a significant early loss, such as the loss of a parent; and neglect.
- **Environmental stressors**: Certain stressors -- such as a death or divorce, a dysfunctional family life, changing jobs or schools, and substance abuse -- can trigger a disorder in a person who may be at risk for developing a mental illness.**(Ref:**

MedicineNet.com

http://www.medicinenet.com/mental_illness/article.htm)

Nevertheless, I'm not here to give you facts on Mental Illness, I just felt it was important to at least help you understand when I share my brief testimony.

For me, I had a nervous breakdown in April of 1998...I'd suffered a great deal of Domestic Violence, I was overwhelmed, DEPRESSED, had just given birth to a baby boy just a couple of weeks prior, I had all 6of the kids home for Spring Break (Step-son included), the baby was screaming and my Ex-husband was screaming. I was mentally, emotionally, spiritually, verbally and physically overtaken by this time. Suddenly my life just fell apart. The longer version is in Part 2 of my *The Silent Screams Series (Someone Almost Loved Me to Death)* but I had a nervous breakdown right in front of my kids, holding my newborn baby in my arms.

I didn't understand that verbally, emotionally and mentally I was already a basket case due to the events that took place in my life as a young girl. No, that doesn't make me CRAZY, it doesn't make me a mental patient per say but we as people need to be careful what we don't allow ourselves to understand. It's was a mental imbalance at that time. I ended up being given all types of depression pills to help me cope mentally and emotionally on a daily basis BUT I didn't take the pills because I realized that as long as I have God, I can come out of this thing. I was determined not to take medicine and feared getting addicted!**(I DON'T ADVISE THIS FOR ANYONE, THIS WAS MY PERSONAL SITUATION).** I was refusing to believe that I had a mental and emotional breakdown from being overloaded. Instead I put my face closer to God, I laid on my face at the altar; the place of slaughter, the place where I can release and leave it at the feet of Jesus. Yes, I had a nervous breakdown even though I had the gift of the Holy Spirit! I broke down mentally and emotionally in my flesh. I can recall before I got ordained Apostle M.J said to us *"if you are getting overwhelmed while dealing with a situation, that means you're dealing with it in your flesh, that if we're giving it to the Holy Spirit, the Spirit knows when and how to shut it down".*

    I realized now that I was dealing with life in my flesh so my flesh had a break down but Glory, be to God for the

Holy Spirit that lives in me. I realized that I had to soon change some things or one day I may have another breakdown and never return to who God purposed me to be.

People understand, emotions can take you to another level. Emotions can cause one to do something that they never imaged themselves doing. We also must understand there's power in the tongue.

Ladies **STOP** teasing that you have bipolar, honestly you just might have it, but not at a severelevel. Stop allowing friends and boy/girl friends to say you are bipolar and schizophrenic and think that it's funny. Someone is suffering from that right under your nose and you aren't aware.

The reality of it all, you might just be bipolar and/or schizophrenic and don't realize it. Stop taking it as a joke and speaking those things into your life; stop prophesying foolishness over yourself **THERE'S POWER IN THE TONGUE!!!!!**

They wanted to put me on Prozac, Zoloft and some other pills but I allowed the Holy Ghost to lead and guide me. There are still days I mustbe careful because my mind tries to shift on me and will shift on me if I'm not careful. That's why it's so important to keep your mind stayed on Jesus. It's so important to feed your mind and think on those things that are pure. **Philippians 4:8 says: KJV** *Finally, brethren, whatsoever things are true, whatsoever things are honest, whatsoever things are just, whatsoever things are pure, whatsoever things are lovely, whatsoever things are of good report; if there be any virtue, and if there be any praise, think on these things.*

We must keep our minds stayed on Jesus because the bible also says in: **Proverbs 16:27-29 TLB** Idle hands are the devil's workshop; idle lips are his mouthpiece.

So, we must be careful allowing our minds to be idle because that's the devil's workshop. There are days that I still get idle and have to quickly shake myself. Personally,**JUST MY OPINION**, we all have a form of mental disorders, just dealing with life in general. Granted some have never gone through anything that would shake their mental or emotional world but 90% of us (if not more) have had some things happen in our lives that's caused us to have to regroup, step back and look at some stuff.

Being in relationships where we've almost hurt someone because of the level of emotional hurt we're in; kids running you insane and you just want to run away and think about coming back later (if ever); the work place becomes overwhelming and you have to walk away and take a cigarette break (for those who smoke), heck some of you had to go take a weed break, hit a line or two, take a drink and pop a peppermint in your mouth and much more. So, most of us have had some form of mental blockage that's crept up on us. To be honest most of us need a dose of medication just to make it through the day. You have leaders that take medication or use some form of boost to make it up on the pulpit on a Sunday morning because LIFE has slapped them over the head. We need to confess and rebuke the spirit of mental dysfunction.

Go ahead and say "Yeap I reckon I've dealt with a bit of mental illness myself" Amen, Praise God it's ok to laugh about it when youthinkabout the truth lol.

Your mind is a place where all kinds of things go on. The enemy targets the mind and will have you wandering and thinking things that are so far from the truth. I remember my former Pastor preached a sermon and talked about how we have full conversations in our minds. How we have full fight conversations in our mind and will have our adrenaline going full speed just by a mental conversation in our own mind. I tell you, when he said that I was just outdone.

We've all had those conversations in our mind OK I'LL SAY QUITE A BIT OF US, BUT I'LL JUST TALK ABOUT ME Amen.

I've had full conversations and even argued in my mind. **I'll give you a couple of examples.**

1. Someone has upset me about something, the person that upsets me, I'm going to step to them AND because I know their mouth is just as fly as mine, I've already rehearsed the conversation in my mind. When I say this, she/he gone say that, and when she/he says that I'm going to say this (and I'm literally having the argument in my mind before I've even spoken to this person) but my adrenaline is up, heart beating face (as if this conversation is going on NOW), I'm all hyped and ready to have that conversation and fight if I have to BUT GOD has a way of causing us to shake ourselves. You end up seeing that person and you're ready to have the real

conversation with the person that you've already had in your mind (SOUNDS CRAZY ALREADY DOESN'T IT) ...when you get to that person and you get ready to say what you've rehearsed...God allows that person to apologize and you never get the chance to say all the stuff you just rehearsed and got yourself all wired up about. DOES THAT MAKE SENSE OR SOUND LIKE YOU? That's how our minds play with us.

2. Your children do something in school, the teacher calls you and you're waiting for them to get home. When he/she gets home I'm going to ask them what did they do today and they gone lie and say nothing and when they lie I'm gone say this and they gone say that and I'm going to get that belt and spank they behind blah blah blah. You're all hyped and just waiting on them to get home, your blood pressure done went up after you've already mentally had the argument or discussion in your mind. The child walks in the door and you're ready, you have the belt on the edge of the couch and you're ready. You ask the child what they did in school and your heart rate is

pumping, suddenly thechild tells the truth and tells their version of it. You've just wasted your mental energy having a conversation in your mind that was never was going to come to pass.

We have to stop rehearsing in our minds because the enemy will cause us a heart attack for something that's not even facts. The bible says in *James 1:9 a double minded man is unstable in all his ways.*

The enemy will cause you to accuse others for something they've truly not done but the enemy will make it appear that way. It will cause one to accuse their spouses of things that aren't true. Even if it's because they have a past that has been shaky but the enemy will cause a situation to look like they really aren't. THE MIND THE MIND THE MIND is a terrible thing to waste but it's easy to waste if we aren't careful. That's why the Bible tells us in **Romans 4:17*"to call those things that be not as though they were"*** speak life in a situation that you can't even see before you. Speak to the dead things and call them alive. Prophesy to your own self and tell yourself that you shall win and that the mind in you is the mind of Christ Jesus.

Mental illness is something I take serious because it's also a generational curse and it transfer from generation to generation. Until you've dealt with a person that has mental illness, you'll never understand. I was married to a person that had mental illness and it wasn't until much later into the relationship/marriage, that I found out that he has issues and that there was a severe case of bipolar and schizophrenia on his mother's side of the family.

Dealing with him wasn't easy and I had a lot of crying days and nights because dude was sick; at that time, I didn't understand mental illness, I just knew he was crazy as all get out. Which while using drugs caused him to be very abusive and almost took my life.

I had kids from him and low and behold, you can't plant an apple seed and expect to get oranges. I didn't understand when his foster mom said to me *"baby be careful of what you allow to be planted into your womb"* I smiled and said ok…ummm you reckon you could've just been up front and said "baby this family have mental illness and it could come out in your children". I had to learn the hard way, after birthing 3 children and watching them go through what they are going through right now (that's another story for another time), but don't take that spirit for granted. Laying down having babies and not finding out the linage of the person you're sleeping with is dangerous and unhealthy. That's for men and women. Men be careful who you plant your seed in because she might be just as crazy as a bed bug also. This is a spirit we can't fight with flesh and blood; we have to fight this thing with fasting and prayer. If it's your individual battle within your own mind you have to fight all the more. Amen

2 Corinthians 10: 3 – 6 says: For though we walk in the flesh we do not war after the flesh. 4 (for the weapons of our warfare are not carnal, but mighty through God to the pulling down of strong holds;) 5 Casting down imaginations, and every high thing that exalteth itself against the knowledge of God, and bringing into captivity every thought to the obedience of Christ 6 And having areadiness to revenge all disobedience, when your obedience is fulfilled. Amen

So, that area of scripture lets me know that we have to cast down imaginations. When the enemy tries to make, you have a full argument/ conversation by yourself, and with yourself in place of the other person, you must cast it down and let the enemy know that you'll go to God and allow the

Holy Spirit to guide you in that conversation when the true person is actually there. Amen

Prayer: I decree and declare in the name of Jesus, your mental state is being restored right now! Go ahead and give God some praise for restoration and redeeming the time. Amen I bind and rebuke every spirit that would attempt to distort, disturb, or disintegrate the development of your personality in the name of Jesus. I break all curses of double mindedness in the name of Jesus; I bind and cast out all spirits of depression, despondency, despair, discouragement, and hopelessness in the name of Jesus! I break and release myself from all curses of confusion and mental illness in the name of Jesus. Amen

CHAPTER 6

Spirit of Suicide (death, dying)

Suicide: the act of killing yourself because you do not want to continue living; the act or an instance of taking one's own life voluntarily and intentionally especially by a person of years of discretion and of sound mind; one that commits or attempt suicide; Self-destruction, self-murder, and self-slaughter. **(Ref. Webster Dictionary)**

Suicide can be onset by many different spirits, leaving you with the feeling that you just don't want to go on any longer. Spirits that consume you to a point where you just don't want to live life any longer. That's a spirit of bondage, mental illness and control (there's more but just my personal experience). Low self-esteem, no self-worth etc.

Whatever one may be going through, it's all connected to a spirit. The spirit of depression had my mind, I was raised being told I was black, dumb, stupid, ugly, never going to amount to anything and no one would want me. Although I grew up by body wise and it appeared I had it all together, I really didn't. I was dying a slow death within and no one knew it but me (now I realize that God knew right where I was during the entire process and I now realize IT HAD TO HAPPEN)

I never loved myself, I had **self-hatred**, low **self-esteem**, I felt I was ugly and all the things that I was told at a young age. We must understand that words are seeds and spirits.

I grew up feeling unloved by the people that should've loved me the most. I was always told I was ugly, not going to amount to anything and no one would ever want me. Being as words are seeds and those words had been planted inside me and watered with the same words almost daily, they begin to grow within me, I begin to live out those words. I begin to believe them, I figured if the ones who should encourage me the most, told me I was ugly and all those other things, and then they had to be right. I accepted that I was black, dumb, ugly and never going to amount to anything.

I felt I had nothing to offer anyone; that I was unlovable and I had to use whatever I had to get noticed. I gave my body away in thoughts that that would make me feel better or at least cause someone to accept me. When using, my body became something that men wanted, I used it as a tool and was still dying inside, but I didn't let it show.

I went through years of domestic violence by my ex-husband who I thought loved me but he was just as lost as I was with no direction, needed me for guidance. He abused me mentally, verbally, emotionally and physically (just as was done as a child void of the physical abuse). I thought I could trust him, I laid in his arms and gave him 90% of my secret pains, only for him to turn around and use all my hurts against me. The **Spirit of Rejection** set in even more. I had children and I felt like I was a failure to them. I smothered my kids because I wanted to make sure that I loved them unconditionally, I wanted to make sure that my children never had to feel unloved by me or anyone. I wrapped myself in my children and wanted to make sure I loved them so much that they will forever love me. Yet my ex-husband was beating me so bad that I wanted to give up.

I wanted to die, I felt like I wasn't worth anything and I was just tired, no one would miss me or even care that I was gone. There were times I thought about taking pills, times I thought about putting the gun to my head and blowing my brains out. I contemplated multiple times driving my car off the bridge, sometimes I thought about doing it with me and my kids because I didn't want to leave them out here in this cold world of people that would probably say to them, the things they said to me OR talk down about me to them, that I committed suicide and left them for others to take care of, then I felt, they deserved better, they deserved to live life and be loved.

I felt if I killed myself, who'd take care of my kids, no one would love them like me, take care of them like me or protect them like me...so quickly I realized that suicide/death was not an option for me. I had to live, I had to get my mind back focused on the Lord.

I had some up and down days, I still had days of wanting to throw it all in and just die. Sometimes when my ex-husband was beating me I used to ask God to let him hit me hard enough to kill me.

When my cousin Brenda promised me that she'd raise my kids and love them if anything ever happened to me, I felt nothing mattered, I could just die now, but I realized my babies loved me, again killing myself wouldn't be fair to them, they didn't deserve that from me.

Suicide is real people and it's a silent death because you're too ashamed to tell anyone what you're going through because people are so judgmental. That's why you can see someone that you've known or not known but shocked that they killed themselves and felt they should've and could've had someone to talk to. Don't judge a situation you've never been in; everyone doesn't have the same resources as you. You don't want people to call you crazy, talk down to you, talk behind your back, think that your issues aren't that bad or say all the normal stuff (it's not that bad; it's not worth it; I know you're not thinking of hurting yourself because of this and that – WELL guess what, it is important to me, it is that bad to me, yes within my mind, I feel it's worth it TO ME). We must be careful how we judge others circumstances, we aren't all built the same. What you can handle, I may not be able to handle and vice versa, but don't judge me because I can't handle what you can. Have some kind of empathy for others and don't be so quick to give YOUR OPINION...what seems simple to you maybe major to someone else.

Be careful how you speak in front of people about situations of others. We tend to sit around and talk about what we'd do if we were in a certain situation, but until you're actually in that situation, you have no clue what you'll do.

I use to say I dare someone to put their hands on me or I'd do this and that but the reality is, someone did put their hands on me, they did it for just over 10 years of my life. When I was in the world, I had 4 guns in my house when the jack boys came rushing into my house and put guns to everybody's head including my 2-year-old daughter. I use to always say "I wish someone would come up in here with all the guns I have, it wouldn't be good". Well I wasn't expecting them to come in when they did. Like the Bible says "Coming like a thief in the night", well the jack boys didn't tell you when they were coming, they just came. With all the guns, I had in my house, when they came in, I couldn't reach either of them; that's when the reality of **DON'T SAY WHAT YOU'D DO IN A SITUATION UNLESS YOU'VE BEEN IN IT;** the reality of being able to know right where my guns were, that one was in arm reach but I didn't have time to grab one, as I was watching someone hold a gun to my baby's head and I couldn't move. Yes, that's reality. After they got what they came for and left, others were saying how if it was them they would've done this and that but the reality was, I couldn't, I didn't have time, it all happened so quick.

You may have a friend or family member that's dying inside and don't have anyone they can talk to and they're afraid to talk to you. I know we tell our friends "Girl/Man you know I'm here for you, you know you can talk to me at any time about anything" but that same friend hears you judging someone else that's in the same situation they're in so now they don't want to talk to you. Have an open heart and mind to receive others and stop being so judgmental just because their situation or sin is not like yours. That's where GOSSIP comes in at. If a person wanted to share with you that they are gay, but they've heard how you talk about gay people, do you think that they'll tell you OF COURSE NOT.

Those of us that declare that we are children of the Most High; you probably need to start acting like it. Have you ever asked yourself **"WHAT IS THE SECRET SIN THAT SO EASILY BESET YOU"**? Your friend or family member maybe crying inside and you're sitting right there and they can't talk to you, then if they commit suicide, you'll be the first to say "they could've talked to me", well maybe they couldn't because they've heard how you judge others so badly but you won't pull the plank out of your own eye.

Take these few scriptures and hold them in your memory bank.

NIV Matthew 4-5 says: *4 How can you say to your brother, "Let me take the speck out of your eye," when all the time there is a plank in your eye? 5 You hypocrite, first take the plank out of your own eye, and then you will see clearly to remove the speck from your brother's eye.***Luke 6:42** *(says the same thing).*

KJV Hebrews 12:1 says: *Wherefore seeing we also are compassed about with so great a cloud of witnesses, let us lay aside every weight, and the sin which doth so easily beset us, and let us run with patience the race that is set before us,*

Stop judging what's not your sin and open your heart to that sister or brother that is inneed of an outlet, that's not to say our Men and Women of God should accept any and everything that comes to them BUT you should have an open heart to allow that opportunity to ministry to that soul that has issues that aren't pleasing to God. I guess you didn't realize that you're in sin for judging the wrong way and don't use that "Christians will Judge the sinners mess", I'm talking about being able to use the opportunity to cause a sinner to repent and trust that you'll lead and guide them instead of condemning them. Amen

So, let's understand that suicidal spirit is real and it doesn't discriminate who it tries to attached to. Determine in your mind that Suicide is NOT an option in your life and that you SHALL live and NOT die. Amen

Prayer: Father God I come boldly to the throne of Grace, asking you to speak to our hearts. Holy Spirit, lead and guide us into all righteousness. Lord let this mind be in me which is also in Christ Jesus. We come against the spirit of suicide right now Lord. I rebuke and cast out all spirits of affliction, sorrow, and anything attempting to bring me low in the name of Jesus. Amen

CHAPTER 7

Pride

Pride: a feeling that you are more important or better than other people. Inordinate self-stem: (**Webster Dictionary**). Although it also defines a feeling that you, respect yourself and deserve to be respected by other people. A feeling of happiness that you get when you or someone you know does something good, difficult, etc. Pride runs in many ways BUT the pride that was revealed in me, wasn't the pride of thinking I was better, but the pride of feeling that I don't need help from others and not trusting other people. Amen

I never felt that I was a person that had pride or felt more important than others. Not until I started asking the Holy Spirit to reveal me to me, to turn the mirror around and let me see me, to circumcise my heart, root out what's inside of me that's ugly and not pleasing to God. When the Holy Spirit said pride, I was taken aback because I've always had low self-esteem, now you're saying pride...I'm confused Holy Spirit. The Holy Spirit began to tell me such as he did with being a liar. "Young lady YES PRIDE", not the pride that you think you're so much better than others but the pride that you don't need anyone, the pride that you'd do without before you ask anyone to help you, the pride where you'd go hungry, your lights will be out and you won't tell a soul because you say it's not their business OR you don't want anyone looking down on you and talking ugly about you. I said to the Holy Ghost BUT WHAT'S WRONG WITH THAT, that keeps people out my business. The Holy Spirit let me know that I've assigned people in your life that will bless you and you're holding up their blessings by not allowing them to bless you! You don't know who they are because you're too proud to be still to see, you don't have a desire to see because you've already set in your heart, mind and soul that YOU WILL NEVER ASK ANYONE FOR ANYTHING and because of that prideful attitude, you can't see the ones that I've assigned to you.

The Holy Spirit showed me where I won't even ask my own husband to do certain things for me because my pride gets in the way, I don't want to feel needy, I don't want him to feel like I can't do it without him, that's why I remind him often that **"Before there was a YOU, I was doing this myself"** and disrespecting that man with your words and didn't even realize it because **PRIDE** had me blinded.

Now I understand where the Holy Spirit checked me with pride...now I need YOU to check within yourself to see if you have that same pride. Feeling like you don't need anyone, feeling like you'll do it all by yourself because there's so many gossipers out there and you don't trust people. Now look beyond that and think of someone that you know, will have your back.

See sometimes we don't ask for help because we've portrayed this "I'm strong, independent and don't need anyone attitude, that we're now, not only prideful, we are shameful. Ashamed to ask the person that's there for you, to help you because you have them thinking you have it all together, when in all reality, you need some help, even if it's to vent. God will put individuals in our lives that are there for us but we don't want anyone to see our vulnerable side BUT those are the ones God has already shown that there's a mask that's hiding some deep stuff.

Pride can even keep some of you from having or keeping a good man or woman in your life because your expectations or too high, even above what you can handle yourself. You expect someone to bring something into your life that you aren't living yourself OR you expect someone to live up to whatever past life you've had and they must endure your mess and they won't so you end up lonely. Within your mind you're saying it don't matter, I don't mind being alone but it does matter because you're lonely but don't want anyone to know it. You know there's a post I saw on Facebook, this guy said "You're always saying you want a man/woman to bring this and that to the table in order to have you BUT you're still renting the table lol, just a bit of humor but it's true.

    We want a man tall, dark and handsome, a woman, thick, nice breast etc. But are you maintained yourself, to handle the request? Ladies is your attitude stink, are you always begging for money, are you conceited and unfriendly, can you carry on a full lady like conversation, is your house clean, can you cook, can he take you to meet his family and you conduct yourself like a lady, DO YOU HAVE A WORSHIP LIFE, TO YOU HAVE A CONNECTION WITH GOD, DO YOU SPEAK IN A HEAVENLY LANGUAGE, CAN YOU REACH THE THRONE ROOM OF

GOD, are you expecting a man to come in and do for you what you can't even do for yourself, have baggage that you want this man to help you carry. MEN...are you balding, pop belly, nasty attitude, conceited, expecting a woman to take care of you, expecting her to have the house clean while you play video games, do you have a job, a car and keep yourselfwell-groomed AND DO YOU HAVE A PRAYER LIFE, CAN YOU TAP IN TO THE ANOINTING OF GOD, WILL SHE EVER SEE YOU WORSHIP – WITH HER? There's so much that we ask for but we aren't maintenanceready or even qualified for what we're asking for. Ask yourself; why haven't you attracted what you're looking for, is it something in YOU that's missing. Come on be realistic, put your guards down. Some of you have good men/ women in your life but you run them off with your stinking attitude or your stinking thinking.

Make sure you've put away your little girl and little boy games of cheating...ladies don't let that man hear you gossiping all the time, talking about everybody and then laughing in their face the next minute, don't go bouncing yourself around his friends when they are around SIT DOWN somewhere. Men don't think it's ok to contact her friends when y'all going through something, that's not cool, all that hugging and being friendly; come on let's first show some respect. Most of all ask God to give you your husband or wife, make sure they have a prayer life and a worship life and that their worship is for real…make sure that He/She loves God more than they love you. Amen

Prayer: Father God I renounce all pride, haughtiness, arrogance, vanity, and ego inherited from your ancestors, over your life in the name of Jesus, I break all generational curses of pride in the name of Jesus.

CHAPTER 8

Hatred & Unforgiveness

Hatred:(Oxford Dictionary) intense dislike or ill will. (Merriam-Webster): a very strong feeling of dislike HATE prejudice hostility or animosity. Extreme dislike or antipathy, loathing.

Unforgiveness: not willing to forgive others; very harsh or difficult: not allowing weakness, error, etc. (unforgiveness brings the family of stress, demonic spirits and toxins).

Well I wasn't surprised when I was hit with hatred and unforgiveness (although it's been some time now that I've been delivered from it). I won't say I knew for a fact it was hate because I try to never hate anyone and try not to hold unforgiveness in my heart for people; I thought it was a very strong dislike and just didn't want to be around these people; but the reality of it was, it was hatred.

You know one can say they don't hate a person ANYMORE as long as they aren't around them BUT when that certain person come around and a form of rage come over you mentally to a point you can say within your mind OR actually feel like you can hurt them for what they did; then you still have stuff inside that hasn't been dealt with.You want them to be punished severally for what they've done to you or your loved ones? You really don't know if you're healed until you come face to face with your hurt.

I won't say I hate the person that belittled me as a child but I had a strong dislike, I didn't show it but I cringed every time I had to be around them and I often thought about the hurt and found myself mentally rehearsing their mean words in my head. Then there was a particular person that made me regroup and stop feeling like I wish something really bad would happen to them. I got to a point where I wanted God to do something to them or a family member BUT I had to understand, that's not how God operate and that was not the God I serve and that's not the kind of woman that God called me to be. Was it easy?NO, it wasn't easy but I had to make some decisions.

The guy that molested my baby, I wanted him DEAD, if it wasn't for my kids, he'd probably be dead today BUT I'd also be in prison, so wisdom is very important. See I say different strokes for different folks; my former Pastor use to say "Grown folk do what grown folk want to do", God gives us choices, HE does not strong arm us into what we don't want to do. The Holy Ghost in me had to make a split-second decision because my flesh wanted to kill him instantly. I had to make a choice to listen and trust the spirit of the Lord or take the chance on losing everything even in the midst of the rage and anger. Trust me, it wasn't ME that stood, I take no credit other than being obedient to the voice of God, But to GOD be all the Glory!

I honestly don't know what feelings I'll have if I ever saw him again because after thatday I wanted to blow his brains out, I never saw him again because he left town. I pray for him, that he's not hurting another family, I pray for him that God will fix him and cause him to repent, I pray for him that if he is doing something to other people that he gets caught and be punished but I try not to linger on it because then my mind will go into another place of flesh that it shouldn't AND it has before. I'd pray that if he's still bothering kids, that he'd go to prison and some things happen to him and because he used God to molest the minds of others, I wanted God to sho nuff deal with him. Nevertheless, I do know that vengeance is the Lord's and he will repay him for what he's done to not just to my child but any others kids he may have hurt and used the name of the Lord to manipulate.

I had to make up in my mind that all the people that has come into my life and caused me to hurt; I needed to forgive them, even if I never talked to them again or see them again, I had to forgive them EVEN if I wasn't the one that caused the hurt. I had to realize that as long as I feel some type away about them or against them, they were still attached to my spirit. I had to decide; if loving God was more important than hating or never forgiving someone. I had to reflect back on scripture **Matthew 6:12** where we ask God to forgive our debts as we forgive our debtors. Which means I've hurt someone too, maybe not to the extent that I've been hurt BUT I've hurt people.Somewhere, somehow, someone out there may hate or have unforgiveness towards me because I was out there in the world doing some stuff that I probably didn't realize and hurt someone else.

Honestly, there's some people I can reflect back on that I intentionally hurt, rather it was for revenge or just plain down did them wrong because I used to be cold-blooded when I was out in those streets, I had no love or pity. I had people fall in love with me and laughed about it. That means right now today, someone probably hates me and I have no clue.

NO, again it wasn't easy but I wanted the full forgiveness of God. It depends on how bad you want the things of God, how bad do you want God to forgive you of your sins, I guess it depends if you feel your sins and hurts towards others where nothing, they were small and they are easy sins to forget BUT sins is sin and because I want to walk upright before God I had to make some hard decisions. I realize everyone's walk is not where my walk is in the Lord and everyone has a different level of WHEN and HOW they deal with things BUT I say to you. God has no respect of person, the same way you used to be in sin and did some things, someone did some things to you, YES they are different things nevertheless, it's still hurtful.

Do I forget what was done to me or my children? of course not BUT I want to be free from the bondage of all my past hurts, I want to walk upright and Holy before God. I want to be able to unmask the secrets sins that try to hide within, I want to stand on the head of the serpent that tries to keep my mind, body, soul and spirit in bondage.

Most of the time, we're hating someone that doesn't even realize how much we hate them, they are like some of us "don't think the hurts results in being hated". Some people allow others to go to the grave hating them, and still hate them beyond the grave, which means that person still has a form of control over you. It's not worth it, they aren't worth it, you deserve to be free from THEM...the forgiveness and release of hatred isn't about them or for them, it's for you to be released from the clutches of the enemy, the residue of them and your past.

When we refuse to forgive, we open the door to demonic spirits. We sit and allow the anger (or whatever the case may be) to fester, and when we allow it to fester, it turns into a spirit or torment to your mind and your body. Now you have a demonic spirit just eating away at your thoughts and your will and before you know it, toxins have set in and now you're releasing the toxins through sicknesses. That spirit is eating at your heart (because someone broke it and the enemy reminds you of it daily), then you open the door to heart attacks; you open the door to body aches because you're warring within. You must understand that unforgiveness will bind you like nobody's business. You can't stand to look at a person, you can't stand to hear their names, you don't like your children because they look like the EX, you don't like the children because they love their other parent that hurt you. All of that is toxin flowing through your body. Then you try to move on and have another healthy relationship (not just male/female, but even a simple trusting friendship). You can't have a healthy relationship if you're unhealthy Amen! So, ask yourself is it worth it, ask yourself have do you have sickness (toxins) going through your body, pains, weight gain or loss, mind all messed up etc. all that could come from that toxic demon that's resting within you and eating at your mind.

Ask the Holy Ghost to show you if you have some hidden hatred or unforgiveness in your heart, ask Him to move it so that you can flow in your purpose. You're wondering why you're stuck at a standstill in the things of God? You might have some baggage that God can't allow you to take on the next level He desires to take you on. Your baggage is too heavy and God is trying to release a new thing in you. He can't release new wine in that old hateful unforgiving skin. Amen

We also have to ask God where was HE in the midst of the hurt that was allowed into your life. Sometimes the very thing that we're angry or unforgiving of, we caused on ourselves. We didn't heed the warning signs that God place before us not to even go that route. Step back and take responsibility of the area you may have played, ask yourself did you have a part in causing your own hurt OR did God allow that hurt in order to move you from that situation and give you better. Sometimes God has to allow things to get real crazy in order for us to let go. If that's your case, then you should be praising God and thanking Him for the release and know it was a God thing and you or the other person had no control of the situation. Understand that forgiveness is different from deliverance. Sometimes you have to be delivered from a situation because that thing was in at the root.

Baby your pain is pushing you into your purpose! Embrace it. Don't allow the enemy to cause other myriads of health issues to set in. REBUKE IT NOW!!!

Prayer: I bind and cast out every root of bitterness, all spirits of hatred, resentment, violence, murder, unforgiveness, anger, and retaliation in the name of Jesus. I cast down vain imaginations and everything that exhausted itself against the knowledge of the Lord. I pray right now that every spiritual demon's that's tried to take root and release toxin in the mind, body, soul and spirit of your people, will be released right now in the name of Jesus! Lord I pray that you will show them that YOU Lord was right there all the time. Cause them to look deep into the hurt and see that you were right there with them all the time. Amen.

CHAPTER 9

Fear and Rejection

Fear:(Webster Dictionary) to be afraid of something or someone: to expect or worry about something bad or unpleasant: to be afraid and worried

Rejection: (Webster Dictionary) the action of rejecting: the state of being rejected:

I lived most of my life with the fear of rejection, feeling that no one would or could love me, always rehearsing the words that had been spoken into my life as a child. The words that I was black, ugly, stupid and dumb, never going to amount to anything and no one would want me. Then from my ex-husband always reminding me that I was fat, had too many children, I was unattractive, on Section 8 and was only worth laying on my back for a man. That a man would never have me as their woman because I wasn't worth it and I had nothing going for myself.

Yes, one can say *"Yolanda look at all you've gone through and all that you've accomplished, girl you're doing good"*; yes, all that sounds good to the outside person that's outside looking in but the person that's living that life daily, trying to pretend that everything is ok, they feel they will never live up to the expectations of what others think of them. Always feeling like they need to be validated by others or afraid they're going to fail at whatever they desire to accomplish.

Oh of course, we should not care about what others think or feel BUT the reality is, when certain things have happened in your life (which I call Root Issues), you can't and never will understand what the other person is going through emotionally or mentally. You can't see with your physical eyes what's in the root of a person; you can only see the surface. Almost like: you never see what the farmers have to do when they musttill the land to prepare it for the fruit to grow. All we see is the fruit and we consider that nice and fresh. You never see how hard the farmer has to work, you never see the digging, tilling, soiling and the tiresome days that's been put into the grounds in order to plant that seed, you never see the watering, the beating of the heat, the cold and rain that the farmer had to endure in order to plant that seedfor it to grow and you never got to see the beginning and you'll never see the root.Just like you never saw the upbringing of others, you never saw or experienced some of the untold things that someone else had to go through. You only see the glory but you've never heard the real story. You see the oil but you weren't there for the beating, the pressing, the crushing and the shaking that got them to that point. You see their worship but you didn't get to see the many tears. Oh, Glory just shout to God right now if you know what I mean. Thank you Jesus!

Everyone deals with hurt differently, some people where talked down to or mistreated and they succumb to the life and become nothing, get on drugs etc.; where others used their hurt as a stepping stone and went higher, nevertheless if they didn't deal with it properly, it doesn't matter how prosperous they appear, there's still some root issues. They may have an attitude problem; they may be rich and defensive, poor with a good heart. You NEVER know what someone has gone through just by looking at them with your natural eye.

Thank God I made it, but it wasn't always easy. I had and HAVE days where I felt that God had left me, I felt that God was nowhere around and that He was allowing me to sink.

I prayed, I fasted, I sought the face of God continually, but there were days that I felt God was nowhere near me, that God didn't love me, He's forgotten about me and I was just as much a misfit to God as I was to others. The fear of NEVER amounting to anything had gripped me and held me hostage for a long time. Yet it was something inside of me that wouldn't allow me to stop praying. There were times I said I was going to stop praying, stop fasting, stop talking to God but I couldn't; I found myself still laying at His feet, I found myself still asking Him to save me from the hands of the enemy. It was truly the Holy Ghost inside of me that kept praying through me because I wanted to give up.

Yes, I had certain people that spoke life into me, others that say they saw something special, unique and God fearing within me, BUT I didn't see it. I'd smile it off and ask God what is it that they could see in me that I don't see in myself.

I portrayed the image that I had it all together because EVERYONE seemed to depend on my strength, no one saw that I was in fear of failing and felt like if I failed they wouldn't love me. No one saw through the mask and the lying smiling face that I felt rejected and only used for what I can do for others.

Yet I didn't take my eyes off God even when I wanted to, I just couldn't. I'd stay home from church and say I'm not going anymore because it was no use, but I missed my time of worship. I missed being in the presence of the anointing that would flow in church and kept me built up.

I procrastinated a lot and I not long ago found out that procrastination is a form of fear. Nine times out of ten, we delay and postpone certain situations, it's because we're afraid or unsure if it will be successful. Once I begin to look back on the things that I pushed to the side and accepted reality; it was truly because I was afraid to fail. My former first lady told me years ago, "Yolanda, I've never in my life seen a person that procrastinate as much as you, you have to break that spirit and move forward, what are you always waiting for", but just recently I realized it was a form of fear.

Today I'm grateful to God that I continued to pray; I continued to fast, but most of all, I had people praying for me that I knew not. I had prayer warriors standing in the gap praying my strength when I was weak. So, don't underestimate that someone doesn't notice you're going through and they stand in the gap for you even if they never say a word. That's why the days I felt I couldn't go on; someone was praying for this ole girl and caused me to push.

I'm grateful to God this day that I made it through the pressing, the crushing, the beating and the shaking for my oil to flow; I made it through the tears, the heartaches and fears. NO NO NO NO, this does NOT by any means mean that I've arrived and made it; but what it does mean is that I acknowledge that NO WEAPON FORMED AGAINST ME SHALL PROSPER and when I can't trace God I have to trust Him, what it does mean is I know God is able to see me through, it means that no matter what comes, no matter what goes, I won't let go of God's unchanged hands and I know that someone is praying for me and I know that fear and rejection is a spirit. I know that I don't have to be afraid of men and their faces. I am who God says that I am. So, when fear and rejection tries to sneak in on me, I bind it quickly and begin to speak what thus said the Lord, I began to declare what God said about me, what my daddy ABBA FATHER said about me.

Prayer: Father God in the name of Jesus, I pray right now that fear and rejection will be plucked up by the root from the mind, heart, body and souls of your people; that you will show them that you are Jehovah Nissi, you raised a banner and have hid them from the enemy and that no weapon formed against them shall be able to prosper. I speak Holy boldness into your people right now. That they will understand "if they are rejected by anyone, that wasn't the person, place or thing that was meant for their lives" that whatever YOU bless, no man can curse. I pray the spirit of procrastination will fall from them right now in the In the Name of Jesus, that they will no longer delay the assignment of the Lord but cancel the assignment of the enemy over their lives. I pray that you will stand in the mirror and speak to the person in the mirror and let them know how much YOU love them. Appreciate them and thank them for never leaving you and keeping your deepest secrets. Love and embrace the person in the mirror. Amen

CHAPTER 10

Doubt & Unbelief

Doubt:(Dictionary.com)to be uncertain; consider questionable or unlikely; hesitate to believe: distrust: to fear; be apprehensive about

Unbelief:(Dictionary.com)the state or quality of not believing; incredulity or skepticism, **especially in matters of doctrine or religious belief.**

For a long time, the spirit of doubt and unbelief controlled my life. Even now I still must bind the enemy when it tries to sneak in on me when trials come at me.

I was a person that believed God could do anything and that He would do anything for everyone else BUT ME. I could and would speak into the lives of others, I would pray for them diligently and watch God move on their behalf but in the back of my mind, I'm feeling some type of way because again, "God you did it for them but you'll never do it for me". When others would come back and tell me thank you for speaking into their lives, for praying for them and how God has moved on their behalf; it does my heart well because I know that God is able to do exceedingly and abundantly above all that we can ask or even think, but just not for me. I doubted everything about me and didn't believe I was worthy.

Even when other spoke in my life, even when it almost felt like I was about to be blessed, my unbelief and doubt cost me. God moves on faith. *Matthew 17:20 NIV says Because you have so little faith. Truly I tell you, if you have faith as small as a mustard seed, you can say to this mountain, "Move from here to there,' and it will move. Nothing will be impossible for you.*

At that time, I believed that I could speak to the mountain but I was speaking to the mountain in vain. I would speak to the mountain and in my mind say "now watch it don't happen for me"and when it didn't, I could say SEE THERE; in all actuality, I wasn't asking in faith, I was still in doubt. I've spoken that "mountain moving faith" to others so many times and they stood on that mustard seed faith; but for me; I still didn't believe it would happen for me. I didn't like to be let down; I was afraid to think further than where I was already standing because I already felt I was a failure. Oh, but how many know that I had to come out of that. I had to find some worth down inside this little girl name Yolanda. I knew that I couldn't just live like this forever and I needed to be an example to my own kids and grandkids one day.

I had to get into a place where I found myself worthy of the mountain moving experience as well. I had to begin to pray and ask God to help me in my unbelief, to help me not doubt who HE is in my life and not doubt the Holy Spirit.

I had to begin to reevaluate my thought pattern and during my reevaluation process I realized that Iwas around negative people that also doubted and didn't believe God would bless them. I had allowed others to speak their doubt and unbelief into my spirit man and our misery was keeping each other company. I had to change my surroundings and begin to speak life into my own surrounding. I had to ask the Holy Spirit to help me because I couldn't do it by myself. The Holy Spirit let me know that my thoughts where as such because I didn't know my own worth. That if I'd see my worth, I'd then see that God loved me and that I was already blessed. I had to take a step back and look at how far God had already brought me from, how much He'd already done in my life; things that I never thought He'd do for me or bring me out of was already done.

It didn't happen overnight but it's happened, I'm stronger and I'm better and I trust God and I don't doubt who He is in my life. I believe that I'm worthy to be blessed, I believe that I am the head and not the tail, I'm above and not beneath, that I'm the lender and not the borrow and that God is able to do just what He said He would do.

Yes, again, I still have days that the enemy tries to sneak in and tell me I'm not worthy and that ugly spirit of doubt and unbelief tries to raise up its head. That spirit tries to visit me through trials and tribulations, with my family and finances BUT God has never failed me yet.

I had to learn how to pray scriptures related to my doubt and disbelief. I had to continue to pray and reverse the curse that the enemy was trying to set before me. I had to call those things that were not as though they were. Amen

Prayer: Lord I cancel the assignment of doubt and unbelief; I pray that you will cover the mind of your people OH Lord. Cause their mind, will, emotions and souls to line up to your Will for their lives. Move in their lives as only you can, reverse the curse of the enemy that's tried to keep their minds in doubt and unbelief and show yourself mighty in the Name of Jesus!

CHAPTER 11

Rebellion & Stubbornness

Rebellion: resistance to or defiance of any authority, control or tradition: the act of rebelling.

Stubborn: unreasonably obstinate; obstinately unmoving like a stubborn child: difficult to manage or suppress: **(Webster Dictionary)**

When dealing with rebellion and stubbornness, you encounter the spirit of **Self-will:** a stubborn or willful adherence to one's own desires or ideas. You run into **Selfishness:** having or showing concern only for yourself and not for the needs or feelings of other people and **Arrogance:** an insulting way of thinking or behaving that comes from believing that you are better, smarter, or more important than other people. You mustunderstand; spirits have family members that come with them and stay even if they're not invited. When one family member comes in, the entire clan comes tagging alone. Amen.

I never thought that I was rebellious but I knew I was a bit stubborn lol. The Holy Spirit had to let me know that I was rebellious. I was rebellious in many areas but mainly my spirit. God will give us warnings even when we are in sin and that's because He loves us so. The spirit of God will unction us to NOT do something, speak to us but because we are who we are, we still do it. My former Pastor would say "grown folk do what grown folk wants to do" and that's pretty much what it was all about. Have you ever saw the commercial or the picture where the devil sits on one shoulder and the angel sits on the other shoulder trying to get you to make the right decision? Well that's where we find ourselves when it comes to the things of God.

There's many of times I've been warned not to do a specific thing but because I was grown, I did what I wanted to do anyways OR there's been times when I feel that unction of DON'T DO IT (even if it was to curse someone out), I'd still do it and my flesh felt good in the end but my spirit was somewhat sad because I did wrong or I'd hurt someone's feelings.

I never realized until the Holy Spirit spoke to me that it wasn't all about ME, it was the fact that I was being rebellious, disobedient and stubborn towards the God. You may wonder where arrogance is coming from in this, the arrogance comes in where you're puffed up, feeling like no one tells you what to do. Rebellion, stubbornness and arrogance are very ugly spirits and you can't go far with those spirits especially in the kingdom of God.

I had to realize that even in my marriage I was rebellious (come on ladies, say ouch)! We're good at saying that we know how to submit BUT ain't no man gone just tell me what to do or run me. Yeah I can hear someone saying right now "well that's true, he not gone just run me". Yeah men I can hear you to "saying naw I'm a man, she not gone just tell me what to do because I oversee the house". Well in a marriage God oversees the man and the man oversees the wife. If the man is in right order with God, He'll lead the woman in the correct direction BUT when we want to throw our authority around, we allow that flesh to supersede what the spirit of the Lord is saying to us in the house. That's why we have division in the home because ORDRE is not in the home. Now don't get me wrong, there are MANY situations where the man or woman is in order with God BUT the other spouse is out of order. Pushing your chest up because you don't want to be told what to do. Your chest puffed up and you want to do what you're big and bad enough to do.

In the house our spouse doesn't want us to do certain things ladies but we still want to do it because "He don't tell us what to do". We must have respect and pull in that rebellious spirit. We want to hang with the ladies but the husband thinks this might be a night that we need to stay in BUT who does he think he is? He's your covering, maybe he sees something in the spirit realm that you don't. Even if he's out of order by telling you not to go for his own selfish reasons, let God deal with him, it's not your job to correct him UNLESS God gives you that open door. God is a God of order and He will bring His correction. **YES, LADIES I KNOW IT'S HARD LOL, BUT YOU CAN DO IT**. Men, you don't want a woman telling you anything, because you were raised in the house where your dad handled everything and your dad ran the house, well was your dad in the right order with God and handling it with the respect of God and how did your mom handle it? Or you're saying "I'm not going to let a woman tell me what to do, I watched my mom run my dad and it's not going to happen with me OR I had a woman in my life that tried to run me and I said that will NEVER ever happen again. Wait, is this woman telling you something wrong; is she telling you something out of the will of God OR are you just stubborn and don't want to hear what a woman has to say? Or are you stuck on "women should keep quiet period" and not just in the church? Come on we must do better men and women of God. We don't want the spouse telling us nothing, we don't want the Pastor telling us nothing, we just don't want anyone telling us anything to do.

Again, it's not that I've arrived lol, I still have to speak to myself and say "back down Yolanda, pull it in, straighten up, God is watching you. See we tend to fool ourselves that just because we're on the pulpit, we don't have these issues. THE DEVIL IS A LIAR, you're human and you have human issues. You just learn to deal with them quicker than the normal person SOMETIMES lol.

Rebellion and stubbornness is the reason some of you don't have spouses or can't keep a relationship. You have all the sense; you know it all. You want things the way you want it and nothing is going to change that, you're not going to compromise. Make sure that you match up to what you're requesting. Maybe your expectations don't match up to who you are. Maybe you should check yourself and stop trying to be in control of everything.

We must learn how to be keep quiet sometimes, the bible says **Proverbs 15:1"a soft word turns away wrath"** and **1Peter 4:8***love covers a multitude of sins*. So how about you give a loving soft work and kill two birds with one stone. Lol You must do better if we want better or you'll stay single to the grave. Go right on ahead and say things like*"So if that's what I have to do, I'll do it; it doesn't matter to me, I like being alone"***STOP LYING** and stop holding up the blessings that God has for your because you're Underqualified for the Overqualified man or woman you're expecting to come into your life. You need to be living right now as if you're married (NOT WITH SOMEONE – SHACKING), BUT live in preparation and stop being so rebellious and stubborn. God is not pleased with you. Come down and accept what God allows, you're better off anyways! Amen

Prayer: Lord help us in this season to release the spirit of rebellion and stubbornness, how well we know that's a spirit of witchcraft and Lord that's not where we desire to be. Lord I pray that your people will humble themselves and seek you more and hear what the Spirit of the Lord is saying to them in this season. Cause us to be obedient to your word God and accept constructive Christian criticism in order to go higher in you. In the Name of Jesus, I pray. Amen

CHAPTER 12

Jealousy, Gossiping and Sowing Seeds of Discord

Jealousy: an unhappy or angry feeling of wanting to have what someone else has. Petty lol, yes the Webster Dictionary said the word P.E.T.T.Y, Petty!!! (the family members that comes with jealousy is covetousness, enviousness, envy, resentment and the green-eyed monster

Gossiping: a person who often talks about the private details of other people's lives(Family members that come: Backbiting: to say mean or spiteful things about (as one not present; Talking behind someone's back)

Seeds of Discord: A lack of agreement or harmony (as between persons, things or ideas) active quarreling or conflict resulting from discord among persons or factions. A harsh or unpleasant sound. (family members they bring are: conflict, friction, strife, war and warfare).

There's so many others ugly enemies that comes with jealousy, backbiting and sowing seeds of discord but I just named a few.

When it came to this I was also confused because I don't be around enough people OR care enough about what others do to be jealous or care to talk about them. The Holy

Spirit had to let me know that one can be a part of each of these areas without realizing it to a degree. We are not stupid; we know wrong is wrong even if we don't open our mouths. If someone is being talked about to you or around you and you don't stop it (or at least try), even if you just listen, you're still guilty to a degree.

I knew I couldn't be jealous of anyone, I've always had to get mine from the dirt (in my thug misses voice lol). The Holy Spirit checked me right there "with your haughty self". I always had the mindset of *"All my life, I've had to get what I needed from the dirt (meaning whatever way I could get it), but such and such seems to always get stuff put in their hands and they are wasteful and don't even deserve what they have"*.

Now; I know some of you will say that's not considered jealousy because it's true or that it doesn't mean that you want what they have BUT, it has nothing to do with wanting what they have, it's the mere fact that you're acknowledging that they have something that **you feel**, they really aren't worthy of getting or not deserving of, they're nasty to people, they don't tithes, don't go to church etc. and why can't you get what you want. It's a form of jealously because you're not understanding, how you have needs, you pay tithes/offering, you give, go to church, love the Lord and it seems you have to work so hard to get everything you desire and this person seems to always get something and never have to work for it. Which takes us to Psalms 37 – Fret not thyself because of evildoers, neither be thou envious against the workers of iniquity. For they shall be soon cut down like grass. LOL I know you're saying "yeah but when because this has been going on a long time". WAIT ON THE LORD!!!

We are to rejoice with others so that we can be blessed, even if we feel they are undeserving, we must understand that God rains on the just and the unjust...yeah yeahyeah, I know, it seems like God rain on the unjust more that the just; nevertheless, that may be the only blessings that a sinner may ever get, because in Hell they MAY lift of their eyes. There are times that God may be watching to see how WE receive others that WE may think aren't worthy. To see if we still rejoice with them.

Gossiping and backbiting unintentionally; that comes in where if someone sees a flaw and they noticed that you saw it as well, they come to youand start to mention it.Instead of you shutting them down, you throw your two cents in and start to converse about a situation you wanted to say something about all the time and when they opened the door to it, you ran in and now you're in trouble with God.

Example: *did you see such and such got a new car? They don't go to church, they don't tithe, they stay in the bar etc. and never give God a tap of time, but here we are fasting, praying, paying our tithes and offering even when we can't afford it, giving to the church when our own area is slacking but we can't get blessed like them.* Now remember, this is even if you're talking to a family member or spouse about another family member or spouse, you're still gossiping and backbiting because you're putting your mouth on someone else behind their backs. You're gossiping. Even if you're not saying anything and someone brings the conversation to you. We need to close our ear gates to the foolishness in this season. We need to put a stop to it right then and tell that other person that we understand they may be unhappy about the situation (even if you did have ill feelings as well), tell that person you're just going to pray but you don't want to get in trouble with God by opening your mouth or sowing seeds of discord about someone when you don't know the full story.

We never know what someone does in their own private time, we don't know why God blesses who He blesses. That's God's business not ours. Yes, the Holy Spirit had to check me and let me know that I've opened my ear gates to mess before and have even went and had a conversation with someone else to see if they knew about what I'd just heard. Not that I was gossiping BUT even if I was trying to find out the truth IT WASN'T MY BUSINESS.

We must learn that we can hurt others with our mouths, words are seeds and our tongue is like a sword. We must realize we have power in our tongues and we can't just say what we want about others or even listen to it. Even if you don't mention it to anyone else; the gossip is already released in your ears and you'll find yourself disliking or judging someone from what another person has said, never giving that person the opportunity to show you who they are themselves. IT'S WRONG. We need to pray for one another because we ALL have faults (that's why I'm writing this book because I'm talking about ME and my issues) none of us are perfect and we will never be so don't fool yourself.

Some of you intentionally gossip, backbite, sow seeds of discord and are jealous of others and you have no reasonto be. Some talk about the Pastors and how they run their church, who they pick for what position, why they don't have what others churches have and so much more and we must remember that God sees and hears all things. Amen

You're jealous of others anointing, youdesire to sing like someone because you don't sound as good as them, you talk about the choir but you won't join it and sing; you steal others testimony because you feel your testimony is not worthy to be told; but testify what God allowed you to go through. HE has assigned someone specifically to you to hear what YOU have gone through in order to bring them out of what they're enduring at that time. Some of you want to preach like someone else or you down how they preach BECAUSE you desire to preach like them. Be who God called you to be, release what God has put in you for the season that HE wants it to be released. Your gift will make room for you. Amen

We must realizeso much goes on in the body of Christ just as in the streets; we have to understand that the Church is made up of people AND sometimes **"HURTING PEOPLE HURT PEOPLE"**I pray your caught that!!!

No, it's not fair but we need to learn how to love the living HELL out of some people. We must love the unlovable. Amen

Prayer: Lord I pray right now in the name of Jesus, that each and every individual will find out who they are in you, that they will seek the Holy Spirit to show them their purpose and no envy others because they are walking according to your will. Help them to pray for others and see them as a soul and not in the flesh in the Name of Jesus Amen!

CHAPTER 13

Sexual Sins

Sex Addiction

Sex: Activity between two people; especially: sexual activity in which a man puts his penis into the vagina of a woman. Intercourse (as anal or oral intercourse) that does not involve penetration of the vagina by the penis.

Addiction: A strong and harmful need to regularly have something (such as a drug). An unusually great interest in something or a need to do or have something. A compulsive need.

Demon: an evil spirit, a source or agent of evil, harm, distress or ruin. An attendant power or spirit.

(WEBSTER DICTIONARY)

This spirit can attach to you in many ways for many reasons. The sex demon is one of the most deceptive spirits there is. When you're talking about a sex demon, you're talking about many different areas and I'll touch on as many as the Holy Spirit gives to me touch on and define as well. Amen

Being molested, raped, seeing things and being introduced to things at a young age, watching certain things on TV, things spoken into our ears etc. We must understand that Satan has to have an open entrance into our lives, there has to be adoorway uncovered by God. Most times the enemy comes and takes over when you're vulnerable, when we are young, pure and uncovered. For me, my little eyes were introduced to things I had no business seeing, ears heard things that caused my little flesh to react to the unknown.

I watched at a young age as other grown folk engaged in sexual intercourses in front of me, the spirit of lust and perversion jumped into my little body at maybe around 5 or 6 years old (I'll never forget that moment because my body felt something that I didn't understand what it was). While those two people had sex, I was there sitting in front of them and unfortunately watched because they assumed I was too young and STUPID to realize or understand what was going on, **YES WHILE THEY HAD SEX** underestimating my level of comprehension due to my age and without knowledge of the spirits being released into my little life; the man handed me money as they had sexual intercourse, he stared into my little eyes the entire time with a smirk on his face that I can still visualize as I sit here and write this book, even at the age of 48 years old; nevertheless, when he finally reached his orgasm, he stared even deeper into my eyes, as he released, my little body jerked when his body jerked, as if he'd released into me, as if him and I were connected sexually Y'ALL BETTER HEAR ME AND NOT TAKE SPIRITS LIGHTLY. *See what I need you to understand is SPIRITS are nothing to play with and when you don't understand in the spirit realm; you'll underestimate the things that go on and can happen in the spirit.* When that man released, he released a spirit within me via eye contact, although he was having intercourses with the woman physically; mentally & emotionally he was perversely having sex with me in his mind, we locked eyes the entire time, and not only did he release; he spiritually released into me. **DEVIL!!!!** So, when certain things happen in our lives (even as children) we may not understand them right then BUT later BY AND BY when certain things occur, we reflect on those things that happened. Amen

PARENTS STOP UNDERESTIMATING CHILDREN BECAUSE OF THEIR AGES! THEY ARE SMARTER THAN

YOU THINK AND REMEMBER MORE THAN YOU CAN IMAGINE!!!! Stop having sex with them children in the bed. My mom use to say "Sleep ain't always sleep and at work ain't always at work" ...I'm a witness because I wasn't always sleep and if you can think back, you were always sleep either RIGHT!!??

When thatdoorway was opened into my little eyes, life and spirit, an entire army of spirits grew within me as I grew older...as I grew older that demon grew older. A spirit of lust came up on me that I didn't even understand and because that wasn't the first and only time I had that encounter of watching grown folk have sex;each time it happened (rather it was with him or other men), and it continued to release a raging sex demon within me.Lust, perversion, masturbation – just to name a few.

My flesh was itching to experience sex but I was afraid because of all the stories of breaking the cherry and the pain before the feel good, but still my flesh craved it; so eventually I succumbed to it. Once I opened myself of to that enemy, all hell broke loose; that sex demon had me so messed up until sex was all I had on my mind; those constant thoughts caused me a lot of problems in my life.

Being promiscuous for so long, sleeping with men because I couldn't be fulfilled properly and thinking I was living the life, having fun, treating men like they treat women **LADIES STOP COMPARING YOURSELF TO WHAT MEN DO.**

One thing you need to remember is: **LIFE CATCHES UP WITH YOU.**

After I slowed my life down and was getting back into the church, I figured I needed to go get a full physical, blood work etc. to make sure everything was ok with and in my body. My doctor determined at some time in my life I had contracted Herpes virus;the doctors told me that they weren't sure if it was from my past life (before I got saved) or because of a cheating spouse that I had (after getting saved) OR from getting sexually transmitted diseases from my ex-boyfriend in the past because he too was promiscuous. Today I'm thankful to God that I am free, healed and delivered from all diseases glory be to God for THE BLOOD OF JESUS!!! I've overcome that enemy BUT that could've been HIV/AIDS and I wouldn't have known which partner had given it to me (I'll go more in-depth later);

Sex, sex, sex, I got pregnant and had my daughter, not long after her birth I got pregnant again, I was barely able to take care of her and ended up getting an abortion. Yes, I killed my baby (murderer, NO I WILL NOT dress it up and make it look good); I'm grateful to God that I've been forgiven, I aborted my baby out of ignorance and didn't have knowledge to the word of God and even if I'd had the knowledge, I was in so much sin, I don't know if it would've mattered at that time. **YES, I'M LAYING SOME STUFF ON THE TABLE** that 99.99% of people, family and friends didn't know about me but because I want people to be healed, delivered and set free, I need them to face their demons, conquer that sin that so easily beset them and force, command, declare and decree that enemy to back off; show the enemy that "when God put me in position, you can't expose me because I'm telling my own story" Amen!

1John 2:16 For all that is in the world, the lust of the flesh and the lust of the eyes and the boastful pride of life, is not from the Father, but is from the world.

LUST: intense sexual desire or appetite. A strong feeling of sexual desire, a strong desire for something or someone, an overwhelming desire or craving, a lust for power, intense eagerness or enthusiasm, something you deeply desire.

You know we've all been here with lust; we've looked on things that caused us to get aroused. Some of you reading this book right now have gotten aroused in just this short time because of what your eyes are reading and the words that are coming alive in your spirit and in your mind, just from paper. Some of you reading right now are connecting to a familiar spirit and you know exactly where I'm coming from.

Some of us have encountered a spirit of lust that you can't even watch certain things on television or you'll get aroused, you can't even see two animals (insect) having sex, without getting aroused (think it's a game if you don't know that spirit personally). Your eyes are the tunnel to your flesh and emotions, which causes the arousal. You see someone kissing, touching etc., you immediately get aroused a spirit of lust and perversion takes over and causes you to think into a zone, causes you to feel some type of way inside because the spirit of lust has come in. We can look on a male or female and our minds begin to wonder and thoughts get out of control. I know someone is saying that this is normal, but **Normal is**:something that's ordinary and not strange. **Abnormal is:** different from what is normal or average: unusual especially in a way that causes problems. Deviating from normal.

Many years ago, a good friend of mine (WHICH IS A MAN OF GOD) told me I had a sex demon on me and I laughed sooo hard at him. I read him good (yeap, although he was a Man of God I still felt we were personal and we were once a sex item), but being friends after many years with no sexual intercourses, we just left it as friends and he was honest with me. I didn't understand his honesty at first and I picked on him with my friend. We laughed and said he said that because when we were together he was never able to handle me sexually so he figured he'd cover himself by saying I had a problem.

Let me go backwards a minute, this guy was in prison and I stayed in contact with him and there are times I'd write him just to entertain him, knowing he's be gone for most of his life, I just figured I'd rise his lil thing since he was there. He was there and he was learning to trust God and got ordained in prison. I would write him and say all kinds of vulgar things that would get him turned on, tell him all the things I would do to him etc. I guess the Lord dealt with him which caused him to deal with me. I didn't judge him in the end for being (as I called it) a so-called man of God wanting me to talk dirty to him. In the end, I was able to turn it around and say Thank You Lord for allowing him and I to connect in such a way while he was in prison so that you can reveal me to him, that he can reveal me to me (I hope you caught that).

I pondered on his statement all the time when I did certain things, although I'd laugh, there was still a bit of a pause in my laughter but I'd shake it off and keep going. Maybe it was the spirit of the Lord revealing to me the truth within.

Throughout the years, his words stayed with me and a part of me cared and a part of me didn't care, I continued to use the excuse that he was a coward and I was too much woman for him. YET the words of my ex-husband kept coming back to me that I was only good for lying on my back. Unfortunately, I'd already embraced the fact that I'd only be good enough to lie on my back and I used it to my advantage. **CONTROL a Jezebel Spirit!**

That sex demon will cause you to be unequally yoked, cause you to marry someone that wasn't assigned to be your spouse and you will find yourself married to the enemy. Find yourself seeking for a divorce or cheating or all the above. Ask me, I've been there done that and it almost costed me my life.

When we are in our flesh and we get involved with people for the wrong reasons, it comes back to haunt us. Yet when we decide to walk away from the sins in our lives and give our lives fully to God, we're now asking God to save us from our bad choices;we're asking God where He's at in the situation but we can't blame God for our choices.

Men you get involved with that woman because of her lips, hips and fingertips and you knew she couldn't cook, she was materialistic and she was a barfly when you met her, but you enjoyed the eye candy, they trophy that was *1John 2:16 The lust of the flesh and the lust of the eyes.*

Now you're in the church and she won't show up, you're trying to walk the straight and narrow and she's still in the bar or hanging with her friends AND probably cheating. Now you think you can fix her, go on a fast to make it better etc.; we must go through with the choices that we've made.

Women, you meet a man because he has a nice car, gold chains, nice looking, good sex game and you already knew he had a bad reputation, you already knew he was a cheating dog but you wanted to show everybody that you can get him, you wanted to be the winner of the prize and you got just what you THOUGHT you wanted. You start catching pure hell; then we do the norm, we turn to God. We get in church; we pray and ask God to get us out of the relationship or save the man. Well it's not always that easy, especially if you've married him. He may NEVER get saved and he might get saved, on the flip side of that, it may take years for him to get in church. He won't tithe, he won't attend functions, everybody knows you're married but never see your husband OR your husband has slept with half of the females at the church (this is vice versa for male and female). Honey there's so much one will go through when you're unequally yoked and go out and pick your own spouse for all the wrong reasons.

So, if you're going through with an unsaved spouse, just hold on to God's unchanging hands until He bring you out or fix the situation. Remember, you made this choice in your flesh! Some of us give our lives to the Lord, get in positions (licensed and ordained etc.) and still must deal with the embarrassment of an unsaved spouse. We see other saved couples sitting and smiling together (although we don't know what limit of hell they've gone through to get their either); single saved men or women are looking side eyed at you and smiling, and we're allowing our minds to wander all over the place imagining what COULD have been, had we made better choices OR even allowing our minds to entertain being with that person. **DON'T DO IT!**

PERVERSION: sexual behavior that people think is not normal and natural, something that improperly changes something, a sexual practice or act considered abnormal or deviant, distorting or corruption of the original course, meaning, or state of something.DON'T ALWAYS THINK

THAT THE WORD PERVERT/PERVERSION MEAN YOU'RE SOME KIND OF FREAK!!!

Masturbation: Erotic stimulation, especially of one's own genital organs commonly **resulting in orgasmand achieved by manual or** other bodily contact, exclusive of sexual intercourse, **by instrumental manipulation,** occasionally by **sexual fantasies** or by **various combination** of these **agencies. Agencies** mean: a business that provides a **service.** A government department that is responsible for anactivity, area etc.

Now let's look at this from the realm of the spirit and flip it. So, if I'm reading correctly (with definition), in order to get an orgasm through masturbation you must manually stimulate yourself (or other bodily contact) and by instrumental manipulations, you have to fantasize or do various MANUAL things to get aroused in order to get an orgasm. Then it says you have agencies that provide you with a particular service...my my my, agencies, are those spirits that come in and assist you with your fantasies, are those the spirits that cause your mind to go into another place in order to reach an orgasm. Lord if I could just teach this thing on paper the way that I feel it. Great God from Zion people don't be deceived. Feel this thing in the spirit.

I know many people have their own view on masturbation and feel that it's nothing wrong with it; Hey I won't be the one that argue with you but read the boldness in the definition. Masturbation will cause you to want oral sex and masturbate over having intercourse with your partner. When you mix lust, perversion, sex addiction in one body, it's like a time bomb when masturbation is at hand. Take masturbation seriously people of God. I know single people feel like they can masturbate and it keeps them from sinning with a direct individual. I remember hearing a sermon of someone that said "if I'm going to repent for getting an orgasm, it won't be because of a toy, it's gone be from the real deal!" and I had to agree with her but I'd been locked into the spirit of masturbation for so many years that it was hard for a man to satisfy me.

I'm going to roll back one quick minute…I was introduced to masturbation at the age of about 10 years old GUESS WHAT – it was by a girl that was about 12 years old that gave me the intro; I didn't understand what she was introducing me to, I just knew it felt funny but in the end, I felt almost good. I was confused, I was confused in two major ways "WHY IS THIS GIRL TEACHING ME THIS, I THOUGHT IT WAS SUPPOSED TO BE GIRL AND BOY (man and woman), so the first person that introduced me to an orgasm was a female. She laid on top of me, had a sock between her legs and grind on me until I felt this weird feeling THEN she turned around and rubbed and felt herself until she had an orgasm Yes at the ripe ole age of 10 and 12, now what has this young girl been exposed to if she's teaching me this. **OH, DEVIL I CAN EXPOSE YOU NOW BECAUSE I AIN'T SCARED AND I'M FREE!**And I'm about to help others not fear you either, they are coming out in the Name of Jesus.

Some maybe wondering if that ever caused me to get involved in a relationship with a female;No, it didn't, but I will say, had I not came from out of those streets, drinking and drugging as I was I doing, ONLY GOD knows which direction I would've taken in the long run (BUT THAT'S ANOTHER STORY ALL IN ITSELF) AMEN!

I could have sex with someone and still get up and masturbate because I got addicted to it. Again, masturbation will cause you to prefer your spouse to use toys on you more than him satisfying you himself. Women once you've entertained and trained your clitoris to react a certain way to your finger or whatever you use, a man can't fulfill you the way you can fulfil yourself; then you leave that man feeling that he's incompetent in satisfying you, especially a man that knows for a fact he can please a woman but it can sometimes cause him to feel less, questions himself or cause him to branch out and get involved with someone else etc. because you've been satisfied with toys, your finger, tongues **YES I SAID IT**, and anything else that you've used to satisfy that certain spot. There are some women after they get that orgasm, they don't want the man to touch them. *LADIES HEAR ME, TELL THE TRUTH AND SHAME THE DEVIL.* **Sidebar:** I've heard women say, they've gotten into gay relationships because another woman knows how to satisfy them and know where to touch them at more so than a man...OR a man can lick on them all night and not have to go inside them. Yes, that certain spot "the clitoris, the pearl as some call it"!!!! You better hear me and take this thing serious.

Ladies you come to the table with all this oral sex on men, feeling like you've arrived. What you're exposing him to is what your hand and mouth can do but you can't fulfill him totally because he's gotten use to a mouth. Yes, I'm sure he gets off (a man can get off by looking at ANYTHING – lol just me being chauvinist lol).Nevertheless, yes having normal sex will cause him to ejaculate OF COURSE because it's stimulation to them, BUT that won't stop him from going to the next female who's going to put her mouth on him the way that he wants it and the way that he's used to having it because that's a better release for him.*Sister girl and brother man, be careful what you bring to the table (bedroom) and then you don't want to serve it anymore. There's someone out there waiting to do what you will no longer do.*

Again, I can raise my hand to the majority of this because I was there. I'm not sharing with you someone else's testimony; I'm giving you ME. It took me 34 year to be fully delivered and set-free from the bondage of sexual sin, the demon of masturbation etc. The spirit took me into areas that one would never imagine unless they've been there. Maybe one day I'll do an all adult workshop on this topic MAYBE lol.

I'm going to merge off this and one day go deeper at a workshop or speaking of some sort. Please don't let masturbation cost you to not care if you ever get married, cause you to neglect and reject your spouse or cause your spouse to go out and seek other places. Amen

Jezebel Spirit in the bedroom:**Jezebel** defined in **Webster Dictionary** says: an impudent, shameless, or morally unrestrained woman. Looking Jezebel up on Google: It says that she was a deceiver, man-hater, un-submitted, power hungry, intelligent and hard worker, Manipulator, Queen Bee, Domineering, Seducer, and the list goes on. I can admit I was that list and more. I was the one that was shameless and unrestrained; I did whatever I was big and bad enough to do. I manipulated men in the bedroom, I controlled and seduced what I wanted, how I wanted it and I controlled everything. I used sex as a tool, I used it to control and manipulate a man to do whatever I wanted him to do and because some men love for a woman to take control in the bedroom, I used that to my advantage. I was power hungry when it came to the bed room. I use to even pull God into the bedroom SHAME ON ME BEFORE GOD. I'd always say *"if God didn't bless me with anything, he sure blessed me with how to control a man in the bed"* I used to say all kinds of things out of my mouth because I was Queen Bee, I was domineering. I could sleep with an entire family of brothers, cousins, uncles and a father and because of my control over them; neither of them would tell the other because I'd threaten not to see them again. I can go to the house where they all were but neither of them knew about the other because I was a person that didn't kiss and tell and they better not tell either, the sad part of it is, neither of them satisfied me but I knew I satisfied them and got whatever I wanted out of them.

My intentions were to hurt as many BOSS men as I could because of the things I saw growing up (which I care not to share right now). I wanted to deceive and hurt them as much as I could.

Yes, I know someone is saying that was cool, that was boss etc. NO NO NO, it was evil, it was wrong, it was deceptive, it was hurtful and it was NASTY. I share this with you not to brag but because someone need to STOP their mess now and for God Sakes stop thinking this is good. It was ONLY by the Grace and Mercies of God that I'm not sleeping in my grave with HIV/AIDS it's only the grace and mercies of God that I'm not dead by the hands of a man, which was almost my destination. My deception and games caused me to meet the man that beat me for 10 ½ years. I played games with that man, I controlled that man sexually and when I tried to walk away, he wasn't having it and was determined to kill me before he allowed me to walk away from him. YES, the tables turned and I almost lost my life. I opened an entirely different door to my family because of games and an ugly spirit. I caused my children to have to live a life of being Witnesses of Domestic Violence, I opened doors not just in my life, but the lives of my children and grandchildren; I'm determined to break the curse of the enemy.

    We can't play with fire and dance with the devil and think we aren't going to get burned. I could've been lifting up my eyes from hell because of my games GLORY BE TO GOD that HE had a plan for my life. Plans to prosper me and give me an expected end. I'm so grateful that someone was praying for me in my ignorance.

I witness these kinds of things everyday as I scroll down the timeline of Facebook, how the many men and women play games or think they are in control with that Jezebel Spirit and wonder why they can't get a good man or woman, exposing your body and then say **"why can't I find a good man"** because you're showing EVERY other man what he would be getting if he chose you. What happened to our dignity and respect?! You say all men are dogs but you present yourself as puppy chow; men say women are no good, you've slept with 3 friends and got caught with each on. GAMES PEOPLE PLAY!!!

Although I was a quiet WHORE, I was still one. I didn't want to be tied down by one man, wanted to do my own thing because I didn't trust to be loved. Oh, Glory be to God for loving and saving a retch like me. Lord thank you for reaching way down in the muck and mire clay to get me out and clean me up.

Others look at me and they don't know my story, see some people give a testimony or write books etc. and people don't believe them because they don't look like what they've been through and God didn't leave them like they found them. I'm so glad that I can bring a few witnesses to the stand because I didn't do females. Sabrina Page-Chandler can almost give you a line per line story about me because she VERY rarely missed a beat in my life of sin (other than before she met me back in around 1983, my cousin Brenda was there to verify some of my deceptions…I can call to the witness stands a couple of others but I know Sabrina and Brenda don't mind me bringing them to the stand and giving their names. Amen! Oh, don't under-estimate the anointing that's on my life. Everybody don't understand my shout, they don't understand my praise, they don't understand my demeanor because they don't know my story.

    I tell you this people, be careful how you gloat about this sex demon…spirits transfer and you'll look at your children and grandchildren and realize that you've transferred that spirit on to them. For some of us we already see it and for NOW we think it's cute (well I use to). We even laugh about "We get it from our parents or grandparents" and think we get cool points. We even watch out children do certain things and we laugh, give them dap or even school them on how to be an even bigger whore; but it's a dangerous game that can cost you your life when you're playing with a sex demon. Domestic Violence and uncurbable diseases are the main thing. Please be careful of these spirits, they are dangerous. You may not see it now but by and by!

Incubus and Succubus Spirits!

Be careful of the incubus and succubus spirits! Those are two dangerous spirits that we take for granted because of how they come "It's a doorway into your flesh". The **Incubus spirit** is an evil spirit that lies on a person in their sleep; especially: one that has sexual intercourse with women while they are sleeping. A spirit that oppresses or burdens like a nightmare. The **Succubus spirit** is a demon assuming female form to have sexual intercourse with men in their sleep.

These two spirits are the spirits that creep in while you're asleep, they are the cause of you having these wet dreams that you find yourself waking up with and your subconscious mind have you thinking it was a good dream because you were relieved in your sleep; when it was a spirit that had sex with you and caused you to wake up wet from an orgasm. Look the meaning up for yourself if you think it's a game. For years, we've been sleeping with the enemy in our sleep. The enemy is cunning, roaming and seeking whom he may devour. Don't get devoured in your sleep.

I wake up every morning and repent for anything that may have happened in my sleeping, knowingly and unknowingly because the enemy will visit you and leave its mess inside of you. As always, I can go on and on but I'll stop here with this. Please men and women of God…stop taking life for granted and see it beyond the surface. God is not pleased, don't get caught in your sin. Please hear me, **Spirits ARE Real!** Amen

Prayer: Lord Jesus I pray right now in the Name of Jesus, that you will touch the mind, heart, body and soul of each amazing reader. Lord we know that you are God and beside you there's no other. Lord thank you for being the bishop of our souls, the lifter of our heads and the keeper of our minds. Lord let this mind be in us that's also in Christ Jesus. Lord help them to be more like you, give them a discerning spirit to be able to discern and detect the enemy when it's coming against them. Help them to overcome the spirit of sexual addiction. The spirit of lust and Jezebel is trying to rise up in the church yet again but we cancel the assignment of the enemy that would try to come in and take control of our bodies in the name of Jesus we pray. Amen

CHAPTER 14

Generational Curses, Familiar Spirits(Sins)

Generation: a body of living beings constituting a single step in the line of descent from an ancestor.

Curse: something that is cursed or accursed; evil or misfortune that comes as if in response to imprecation or as retribution.

We need to understand that some of us (most of us) are living under a curse that had nothing to do with us directly. It's a generational curse, a curse that may have taken place hundreds or thousands of years before we were even born or even our parents were born. These generational curses of lust, deception, greed, whoremongers, THOTS as they are called today lol, Jezebel spirit and so forth; that curse may have started with our ancestors and runs into our bloodline by default. You know how you have certain family members that say "Chile it's in our blood", Chile you know us Lee's crazy and have zero tolerance etc." Then we laugh and say I heard grandma such and such (or another family member) was off the chain, had zero tolerance and would cut you or curse you out (that's just an example I'm using that I've used in my family linage Amen). We laugh about it but the reality is, WE ARE CURSED with a CURSE because of our bloodline.

We need to understand, some curses we've caused on ourselves. Deuteronomy 27 talks about the many curses (NOT ALL but many) and God is so serious about curses.

Deuteronomy 27: 16-26

[15] *'Cursed is the one who makes a carved or molded image, an abomination to the* LORD, *the work of the hands of the craftsman, and sets it up in secret.'* **Make sure some of your precious possessions from grandma, momma, and other family members was not used towards witchcraft.**

[16] *'Cursed is the one who treats his father or his mother with contempt.'* **Don't disrespect your parents or grandparents.**

"And all the people shall say, 'Amen!'

[17] *'Cursed is the one who moves his neighbor's landmark.'* **Don't bother your neighbor's property or things (even spouses).**

"And all the people shall say, 'Amen!'

[18] *'Cursed is the one who makes the blind to wander off the road.'* **Don't intentionally lead someone astray.**

"And all the people shall say, 'Amen!'

[19] *'Cursed is the one who perverts the justice due the stranger, the fatherless, and widow.'* **Don't pick at people that are not like you, not where you're from or less fortunate than you, ones who's alone without their father or spouse.**

"And all the people shall say, 'Amen!'

[20] *'Cursed is the one who lies with his father's wife, because he has uncovered his father's bed.'* **Sleeping with family members, rather male or female, don't sleep with your step-parent out of the spirit of lust and perversion.**

"And all the people shall say, 'Amen!'

[21] *'Cursed is the one who lies with any kind of animal.'* **You'd be amazed at the stories that are told from back in the days and in those prisons,and back in the country. If someone keeps it real, they've heard the stories about their uncles and other family members having sex with the chickens back in the old days (and maybe even now), I've heard someone that was in prison talk about how on the farms, there's chickens and how the inmates would sneak and have sex with the chickens…OH but it goes deeper than that but we'll stop here. Things like this still happens and it could just be in your lineage.**

"And all the people shall say, 'Amen!'

[22] *'Cursed is the one who lies with his sister, the daughter of his father or the daughter of his mother.'* **Incest in the family, that's a curse all in itself but that doesn't stop that spirit from attaching to you as well, this includes step sisters and daughters.**

"And all the people shall say, 'Amen!'

²³ *'Cursed is the one who lies with his mother-in-law.'* **Think it's a game men, to say your mother-n-law is fine and you'd sleep with her and vice versa ladies.**

"And all the people shall say, 'Amen!'

²⁴ *'Cursed is the one who attacks his neighbor secretly.'* **Talking about your neighbor, killing is another word for backbiting, gossiping, can we say OUCH, the Lord said in His commandments to Love thy neighbor's. Neighbor could also men friends, Associates, church members etc. Amen.**

"And all the people shall say, 'Amen!'

²⁵ *'Cursed is the one who takes a bribe to slay an innocent person.'* **Don't let someone bribe you into hurting or killing an innocent person with your words; stop disliking someone because your homeboy or home girl don't like them and they've never done anything directly to you. You can murder with your tongue. REMEMBER THAT!!!**

"And all the people shall say, 'Amen!'

²⁶ *'Cursed is the one who does not confirm all the words of this law by observing them.'* **Don't get yourself in trouble by not following the laws of God by listening to man. Here what the spirit of the Lord is saying. Amen**

"And all the people shall say, 'Amen!'

I know this is a touchy conversation for many BUT; graven images, (jewelry, candles, ceramics, precious stones etc.), we like to hold on to family air loams that maybe cursed. We like to hold on to things that our momma, grandmamma, grand-daddy, auntie etc. has handed down from generation to generation and that thing may be a cursed, they may have spoken all kinds of spiritual witchcraft over those items.

Rather we want to believe it or accept it, most of our family dealt with some form of witchcraft back in the days. Heck even I must admit that I've dabbled in witchcraft before, call myself trying to get rid of a man that I no longer wanted in my life, as well as a man I wanted to stay in my life and even used it for people that was going to court and needed me to stand in the gap, but I was standing in the gap in sin because I didn't know any better. I watched witchcraft being used as a child so I felt nothing was wrong with it. Especially because they told me to use scriptures out of the bible. Come on how crazy is that??? You're dabbling in witchcraft and yet saying scriptures from the bible. Oh, my, what a curse. **REPENT!!!** YOU need to repent if you've ever been involved in any form of witchcraft (candle lighting, roots, voodoo, Ouija board, séance, palm readers, horoscopeetc.) We should believe the report of the Lord, not witches and warlocks.Break the curse off your bloodline, it is NOT in your blood anymore to do wrong, IF in fact you've been redeemed by the Blood of the Lamb, that means your DNA is **J.E.S.U.S** Amen

Ask God to forgive you for touching that stuff, release yourself from that curse; even if you've sat around and watched it, inquired about it etc. **REPENT**

Same as for the,**familiar spirits**: a spirit or demon that serves or prompt an individual; the spirit of a dead person invoked by a medium (spirit) to advise or prophesy.

Watch out when someone that you have no clue about can so easily attach to you and you say "Oh we are so much alike" ummm well, that's not always a good thing if it's a negative alike. You know how we meet that female that's gutter like we are (USE TO BE) and we think it's cool because BABEEE we are too much alike lol. I've heard people in the church say "Oh we have like spirits" but we must be careful what familiar spirit we embrace into our bosom;I'm not saying that ALL familiar spirits are a curse but it does mean that, that spirit is familiar with you and it's important to see how; just make sure it knows you in a good way and not one of those OLD spirits that come to unbury that old man/woman. Amen!

Those old spirits will come back and cause that flesh to act up. The enemy will send someone into your life to wake up some stuff if we're not careful.

The bible says in Matthew 12:43-45 and Luke 11:24-26

An Unclean Spirit Returns

43 "When an unclean spirit goes out of a man, he goes through dry places, seeking rest, and finds none. 44 Then he says, 'I will return to my house from which I came.' And when he comes, he finds it empty, swept, and put in order. 45 Then he goes and takes with him seven other spirits more wicked than himself, and they enter and dwell there; and the last state of that man is worse than the first. So, shall it also be with this wicked generation."

That lets us know that we must be ready…although we get the spirit out, we must stay clean because it will come back and try to get in and it brings with them seven (7) other spirits. They get in through familiarity, that's why it comes back to where it's lived for a long time and it knows that body but you must be covered under the blood and know that no weapon form against you shall prosper. Amen

Prayer: Lord help them to keep their hearts and minds clear and their souls and spirits cleaned from allowing the enemy a doorway. Lord prepare their hearts and mind to be focused and alert to the tactics of the enemy. To know that the enemy comes like a thief in the night and that they will be ready. In the Name of Jesus. Amen

JESUS HEALING IS NOT RESTRICTED BY TIME, HE LIVES IN TIMELESSNESS, OUTSIDE OF TIME. JESUS HAS BEEN PRESENT IN EVERY SITUATION IN YOUR LIFE. HE IS OMNIPRESENT!!!! OH, GLORY I LOVE YOU JESUS!

CLOSING REMARKS

As I prepare to close these Chapters (until God speaks further). I want to thank you all for taking the time to read this piece of information that I've shared with you; I pray that this information was helpful to you and for you. Yes, I know that I could've got more in-depth and I wanted to get more in-depth as well lol but the Holy Spirit didn't give me permission and I HAD to be obedient to the voice of the Holy Spirit. I'm sure in due season (if it's the Lords will) I'll do and updated version, workshops and/or speaking's concerning this book.

It's been an awesome experience revealing some of my old issues that caused sin to be in my life, it was also a healing session all the more to be able to expose the devils that tried to hold my life in a prison and I pray that the shackles began to fall from your life as well.

I love you all with Agape love, you are my sisters and my brothers in Christ and I pray you many blessings and I pray that you will continue to face your enemies and not be afraid. I pray that you get in touch with your History as Apostle Mark Jones once said (Until we face our history, we'll stay in bondage – the devil is a liar). Face your history and don't be afraid of men and their faces.

Below I've listed some good books that I've read and they may be helpful to you as well. I've also listed below some of the spirits that come with suitcases when the enemy comes (remember those 7 more spirits that the enemy brings to take up residence with you?).

A good book to read is by George Bloomer:The Little Boy in Me.

This is an outstanding book for men and women to read.,*This book exposes those elements that hold men back from becoming the true men of God they are intended to be. Bishop Bloomer offers godly insight on how to overcome those elements.* George Bloomer talks about how he was introduced into sexual sin by an older female that pretty much violated his youth. It helps to better understand why some men may react as they do; **NOT ALL**

but some. You know I always say **"There's a ROOT ISSUE behind ones' actions.**

Strongman - Spirits
By: Jeff and Carol Robeson
Prayers that Rout Demons
By: John Eckhardt
Stronghold's and the list of their family members that comes with them. By: Paul & Claire Hollis, Ph.D.

Revelations 1:3 says "Blessed is he that readeth, and they that hear the words of this prophecy, and keep those things which are written therein: for the time is at hand.

Unmasking

the Secret Sins Within

(The Sins That So Easily Beset Us!)

www.yolovercome.com
Yolanda@yolovercome.com

Author: Prophetess Yolanda Lee~George

Other books by:
Prophetess Yolanda Lee~George

The Silent Screams Series

Part I – Someone to Love the Little Girl in Me

Part II – Someone Almost Loved me to Death

Part III – There's A Stranger in my house!

www.ingramcontent.com/pod-product-compliance
Lightning Source LLC
Chambersburg PA
CBHW071228090426
42736CB00014B/3006